BY DOROTHY CARUSO

ENRICO CARUSO

HIS LIFE AND DEATH

SIMON AND SCHUSTER

ABOUT THE APPEARANCE OF BOOKS IN WARTIME

A ruling by the War Production Board has curtailed the use of paper by book publishers.

In line with this ruling and in order to conserve materials and manpower, we are co-operating by:

1. Using lighter-weight paper, which reduces the bulk of our books substantially.

2. Printing books with smaller margins and with more words to each page. Result: fewer pages per book.

Slimmer and smaller books save paper and plate metal and labor. We are sure that readers will understand the publishers' desire to co-operate as fully as possible with the objectives of the War Production Board and our government.

MANUFACTURED IN THE UNITED STATES OF AMERICA
BY AMERICAN BOOK—STRATFORD PRESS, INC., NEW YORK

Because Enrico
so deeply loved her
I dedicate this book
to the memory
of his mother

THE PHOTOGRAPH which appears on the jacket and as the frontispiece is reproduced through the courtesy of the photographer, Kaiden Kazanjian. The remaining photographs were supplied by Dorothy Caruso and the Culver Service.

THE CARICATURES which appear throughout the book were all drawn by Enrico Caruso, with the exception of Dorothy Caruso's portrait of her husband as Don Alvaro. All of the drawings except "Caruso Making a Record" originally appeared in the Italian-language newspaper, La Follia di New York, and were later used in several editions of Caricatures by Enrico Caruso, published by Marziale Sisca. They are reprinted here by special arrangement with Mr. Sisca.

Contents

Illustrations

PHOTOGRAPHS

viii

Foreword

IF I DO not begin my story in the usual chronological way, it is because I have chosen a moment in time from which I can look backward and forward as if I were standing in a doorway between two familiar rooms. It is the story of two lives that merged into one life, and it is that life of which I write.

The letters of Enrico to me are as much a part of the story as that which I have written. I have left them in the form in which he wrote them. They are misspelled and touching, full of humor and sadness and old wisdom. At times they are curiously Biblical.

I was twenty-five when I married Enrico and twenty-eight when he died. When I write of us I am again twenty-five years old, living once more our splendid tragic life.

Dorothy Caruso

HOW HE LOOKED

OFF STAGE

This was Caruso's first published photograph taken when he was 19. Since his only shirt was being washed, he draped himself in a bed-spread to receive the photographers. See page 143.

Caruso as he looked when he left Italy to come to America in 1904 for his first season at the Metropolitan.

Entrance to the park of the Villa Bellosguardo at Signa, Italy. This gate was broken down by the Revolutionists. See page 35.

Caruso arriving in New York in November, 1913 from his last season in Austria and Germany.

Gloria at the time of her christening. Although she was given five names, her father always called her Puschina.

Caruso with the old Italian comedian, Gravina, at the stage-door
of the Metropolitan. In the background are his tall secretary,
Zirato, and his accompanist, Fucito.

Singing at Sheepshead Bay, September, 1918.

From the train window at Monterey en route to Mexico City.
September, 1919.

Caruso and his valet, Mario, in the studio of the house he took in Mexico City for the Autumn opera season of 1919.

At Easthampton, July, 1920.

Enrico drawing his caricatures at the Southampton Fair, August 3, 1920. See page 207.

This snapshot picture of Enrico was taken at the Vanderbilt Hotel in New York City, February, 1921, while he was convalescing after his first illness.

Enrico and Gloria aboard the S. S. President Wilson, May 28, 1921. This was Caruso's last voyage.

The last picture taken of Enrico, on the terrace of our hotel in Sorrento, a week before his death.

CABLE ADDRESS
"SEVILLA"

TELEPHONE
A-2101

I 10 a.m.

HOTEL SEVILLA
HAVANA
CUBA

Sunday
May 16 - 1920

My own Doro darling

Few words in hurry because
as I have a mattiné. The time
will fly in making my
toilet and prepare my self
to fight again with the public
which is not the same of the first
night been the mattine special subscription.
I had a good night and I feel
rested but I dont yet try my
voice I hope will be allright.
And you dearest, How are you?
I imagin little tired after
all this truble which you had
in New York! And your cold

Facsimile of Caruso's handwriting.

Dorothy Caruso. New York City, 1943.

ON STAGE

Caruso at the age of 22 as Turiddu in *Cavalleria Rusticana*. Italy, 1895.

In the title role of Charpentier's *Julien*.

As Nemorino in *L'Elisir d'amore*.

As Samson.

As Rodolfo in *La Bohème*.

As Canio in Pagliacci.

As Dick Johnson in *The Girl of the Golden West*.

As Cavaradossi in *Tosca*.

As Eleazar in *La Juive*.

As the Chevalier des Grieux in Manon.

As Radames in *Aïda*.

This is the Julien costume that Enrico wore the first time he came to dine at my father's house. See page 44.

ENRICO CARUSO
HIS LIFE AND DEATH

Chapter One

WE HAD been driving all day through the hot dust of August over the long road between Florence and Genoa. Once we stopped in the shade of a pink house painted with pale frescoes and ate a watermelon. Enrico, who was born in Naples and loved Italian summers, looked cool and in order. He smiled sympathetically at my hot crimson face and said that before sunset we would be coming into the fresh air of the port.

The car we were driving was old and noisy, but it was the only one the revolutionists had left us for the journey to Genoa. We were sailing for America the next day because it was no longer possible to live in our Tuscan villa. Although the war had been over for nearly a year, there was no internal peace in Italy in the summer of 1919. After a series of general strikes and food riots, the country had turned against the government and was now in the state of sporadic revolution which was to result, two years later, in the march on Rome.

Unrest had spread even to our little town of Signa, forty miles from Florence, noted before the war for the industrious ways of its inhabitants. The men had always worked late in the vineyards, cultivating grapes for the celebrated Chianti wine; the women and girls were never seen without a package of straws under one arm and a strip of braid running through their fingers, busily weaving the fine leghorn hats that are famous all over the world. Six hundred of these peasants, now sullen and hungry and without work, had come to the villa, broken down the iron gates

35

and demanded our grain, wine and olive oil, which were stored in the cellars. Enrico received their leader and asked for their right of search from the mayor. "We are the mayor," they answered. He didn't argue but merely said he would appreciate their leaving us one of the cars and enough food for the next ten days, after which time we would be sailing for America. They were going to take our poultry, too, until Enrico told them about my white peahen—she was setting on twelve eggs, due to hatch that day if she wasn't disturbed. Their muttering broke into laughter. "The *signora* is a peasant like us," they said, and left without going near the poultry farm. They carried away the oil, wine and grain in carts flying red flags and sold everything for whatever the hungry people could pay. Later they sent us this money—a pitiful little bag of coppers—with a dignified note of regret and gratitude.

Because of Enrico's assurance and resourcefulness I hadn't been frightened by our local revolution. Two weeks before I had had another example of his calm strength when facing catastrophe. At midnight the ferocious white watchdogs that guarded the villa began to clank their chains and howl like wolves. Ten minutes later my bed shook violently. I turned on the light and saw the walls twist. Enrico called from his room, "Come, Doro, stand under the portal here where the walls are thick. It is the earthquake." We stood together in silence, listening to objects falling all over the house. Then he said, "The floor and ceilings may go—the doorways will remain. Or perhaps you prefer the garden?" I had a vision of the earth opening—"No, let's stay here." "Good." He communicated his strength to me and I received it without any exchange of unnecessary words. We never needed words. We understood better without them.

The earthquake was followed by a terrific hailstorm. In Flor-

36

ence rows of houses were destroyed, but our villa was undamaged, except for jammed doors and windows. The next morning we found under the cypress trees in the park a soft carpet of little dead songbirds beaten down from the branches by the storm.

* * *

We had spent such a disquieting summer in Signa that I didn't altogether regret our sudden departure, although I loved the Villa Bellosguardo. It had been built in the fifteenth century on the crest of a hill within a park of pools, statues, formal gardens and long avenues of ancient cypress trees. The avenues led to balustraded belvederes, each with a different view of Tuscany; the one of Florence and the river lying in a mist many miles away was the loveliest vista I have ever seen. The property was so vast that we had no close neighbors, and the outside world came to us only through the sleepy sound of an old monastery bell five miles away.

Enrico bore all the expenses of the estate and in addition gave the farmers half the produce of the land in return for their labors. When he was away from Signa he left the villa in charge of Martino, his old valet, who had been in his service for twenty-two years and had recently been promoted to the position of major-domo. Nothing in life mattered to Martino but the comfort and happiness of his idol.

Enrico had been studying *La Juive* all summer, and many new songs. His accompanist came every morning from Florence and they worked in the music room for three hours. In the afternoon Enrico amused himself by building the scenery for an enormous crèche for which he had bought five or six hundred figurines some years before at the Paris Exposition. They were more than two hundred years old and were dressed in costumes made by the ladies-in-waiting of the Queen of Naples, at the time when

37

the Kingdom of Naples and the Two Sicilies still existed. The stage had been built in the room next to the chapel; it was twenty feet long and stood two feet above the floor. I couldn't stay in this room long without feeling ill—he worked with hot fish glue, and even with the doors and windows open the fumes were over-powering.

I was often lonely at Signa, though never alone. Twenty-one people lived with us; a few were guests, the rest relatives. At first I couldn't tell them apart, as I spoke no Italian and they knew no English. Enrico's two sons, Fofo and Mimmi, joined us, ac-companied by Mimmi's English governess, Miss Saer, who had brought up the boy and adored him but was so frightened of Enrico that she never dared address him above a whisper.

I recognized Giovanni as Enrico's brother because he looked like a caricature of Enrico. In character there was no resemblance between them; where Enrico was open and good, Giovanni was closed and false. He detested me but was careful to hide his feel-ings when Enrico was present.

Donna Maria, their stepmother, was an intensely religious old lady of seventy-five with beautiful white hair. She spoke her native dialect with such an accent that even Enrico had difficulty in understanding her. She worshiped him, distrusted everyone else and hated Giovanni. Once when she and he were having a violent quarrel, he became so enraged that he snatched his straw hat from his head with both hands and bit a large piece out of the brim.

Fofo, Enrico's elder son, was twenty-three, had been a private in the army and was still in uniform. He was blond, short, broad but abnormally thin; weak, surly and given to weeping bitterly at table. Mimmi was a large heavy boy of fourteen, dressed in a white sailor suit, and always with his governess. His voice was changing and he had big hairy legs and a slight mustache. He was

38

a bright boy, but had not been allowed to play with other children and had spent most of his childhood in England with Miss Saer. Enrico's only comment was that he used to be beautiful and that his governess still put on his shoes and socks for him. I thought that he had been under her influence long enough and suggested that we take him back with us to America and put him in boarding school. At first Enrico refused, but when I assured him that the boy would be no trouble he consented and we didn't discuss the matter again. Enrico never vacillated after he had made a decision. He waited for results.

In Catholic Italy, children born out of wedlock have a legal status, provided the father recognizes them publicly. The fact that the boys were Enrico's natural sons, to whom he had legally given his name, and that their mother was living in South America, had never troubled me. The greatest proof Enrico ever gave me of his deep trust in my understanding was when he asked me, soon after we were married, to go to the bank and send the mother of the boys her monthly allowance.

I never discovered the exact relationship of many of the other people—known or unknown to me—who lived with us in Signa as a matter of course, since Enrico was head of the family. I never asked him if he liked having them, because I never asked him unnecessary questions. We all ate in a great ceremonious banquet hall, a beautiful and imposing room. The relatives ate mountains of spaghetti and steaming caldrons of codfish; we had little cups of clear bouillon and the white meat of chicken. I sat next to Enrico, as usual. Even when we dined out in New York he always asked our hostess if we might sit together—"Else, dear madame," he would say, "we cannot come. You see, I can sit by her if we stay at home and I married Doro to be near her."

Enrico's other valet, Mario, served only us at table in the villa; other servants served the relatives. This was strange and pleasant.

I liked Mario. Seventeen years before he had been a railway-station porter. Enrico had been pleased by the way he carried his bag and had asked him immediately if he would like to work for him. Since then they had been all over the world together. Early in the summer Mario told me that he had been engaged to Brunetta for nine years but that the *signor commendatore* wouldn't let them marry. He begged me to speak for him—"because now the *signor commendatore* is so happy with his wife." When I asked Enrico he frowned. "No," he said, "no man can serve two masters. The wife of my valet would be the head of my house, and I would have no valet." I asked him again after the peasant uprising and he yielded. "Mario may go three days before us if he wishes to marry. Then he and his wife will meet us on the boat. But I don't wish to see or hear of her. In America she will be your responsibility." As he turned back to his desk he added, "And remember—no babies."

* * *

The car slid down the steep cobbled streets of Genoa, across a labyrinth of tracks to the port; then on to the pier, piled high with boxes of spaghetti and barrels of olive oil. Mario was wait-ing for us on the dock and opened the door of the car. "Thank you, *signora*," he whispered. "She is hiding in my cabin."

The *Dante* was an unpretentious little ship, but we had the captain's quarters and our own small deck. During the voyage I saw no one but Enrico, my maid Enrichetta, Mario and Mimmi.

Sitting day by day on the little boat deck, I tried to put my confused thoughts in order—so much had happened to me in so short a time. Just one year ago I was still living in father's house, where I had been ever since leaving the Convent of the Sacred Heart. Until that year—I was seventeen—I hadn't known my father well. When he had married my young mother he was a widower with three children, and he was past forty-five when my brother, their first child, was born. After my birth, sixteen months later, mother was always delicate, and as a child I don't remember seeing either of my parents except at breakfast and in the evening to say good night. My childhood was spent in the nursery with my brother and our nanny, who watched over and loved us until we were old enough to go away to school. During those years I learned that father had been graduated from the United States Naval Academy in the class of 1867, that he had served under Admiral Farragut during the Civil War, and that before he was twenty he had resigned from the Navy. At twenty-eight he was editor of the *Scientific American* and a few years later began to study law. At the time of my birth he had become a brilliant patent lawyer, an authority on naval matters, the author of important books on electricity, and a good amateur portrait painter.

In the early years of their marriage mother and father gave beautiful dinner parties for their friends, among whom were many great scientists and inventors. Although at that time I was too young to meet them, I remember some of the famous names —Admiral Dewey, Admiral Fiske, Admiral Seabury, the amazing genius Steinmetz and Professor Michael Pupin, great physicist and inventor, who had been born on a peasant farm in Serbia. He had reproduced that Serbian farm on a magnificent scale at Norfolk, Connecticut, and one summer father took a house in the neighborhood. The professor loved children, and I spent hours with him, listening to stories of his homeland and walking with him through the fields. His hobby was raising black cattle, and one day while we leaned over the fence, watching his herd he said, "Look at those animals and remember that the greatest scientists in the world have never discovered how to make grass into milk." That night I wrote this verse for him:

It's funny how worms can turn leaves into silk
But funnier far is the cow:
She changes a field of green grass into milk
And not a professor knows how.

By the time I was eleven mother had become an invalid and could no longer live in New York; the doctors decided that she must go to the quiet country away from us all. My brother was sent to boarding school and I to the Convent of the Sacred Heart. After I had been there four years it was decided that I would keep house for father, since both my half sisters had married and he was alone. The years of worry over mother's health and the responsibility of five children must have embittered him, for there was nothing left of the popular, amusing and affectionate man whom my sister had often described.

From my untroubled and uneventful life in a convent, I came into a home of strain and tyranny. It must have been trying for father to place his orderly house in my inexperienced hands, and the ideas of a young girl could not have been interesting to a man of his knowledge and gifts. Yet had he loved me he might have borne with me. Unfortunately he didn't even like me, and his impatience was unconcealed and uncontrolled. I couldn't explain his dislike of me except that I bored him. He had a violent temper and I soon learned that he was unreasonable, blustering and egotistical. He dominated and terrified me and was so contemptuous of ordinary people that he would allow none of my friends to come to the house. In these later years of his life he saw his own friends only at the University Club, but he never brought them home to dinner. When he returned from the office at night, the sound of his key in the front door made my heart pound. From the hall he would roar out his desires—steak for dinner—and if lamb had been ordered instead he would stamp up the stairs, shouting accusations that I was deliberately trying to starve him. He exploded into angry sarcasm whenever I was ill; he berated me when President Wilson didn't agree with his opinions; he blamed me for the servants' shortcomings and glared at me across the dining-room table. As he took no interest or pride in my appearance, he allowed me only the most meager wardrobe —and that with such ill grace that at last I never asked for anything I could do without. I had to sit with him every evening in the library, too frightened to speak, yet afraid that my silence would provoke another outbreak of fury.

After a year he could no longer support, alone, my trembling presence and he invited my cousin's governess, Miss B., to come and live with us. She was an Italian woman of thirty who sang. Although father announced that she was to be my companion, I soon saw that her role was to amuse him. With delight he listened to her sing and she listened to him play the pianola. He would pump and pump for her. Since they both loved music and, according to father, I didn't, he took her with him to concerts and the opera. I had heard only one opera, *Lohengrin*, when I was eight years old, and no concerts at all. I had no money for opera tickets and father had refused my timid appeal for a small allowance. One night after returning from a performance of *Carmen* at the Metropolitan, father clarioned his satisfaction for two hours. So the next day I took out of his bibelot cabinet a little silver windmill and sold it for a dollar to buy standing room for the next matinee of *Carmen*, and thus saw Caruso for the first time. But I was too frightened by what I had done to enjoy the singing, and came away unimpressed.

Miss B. diverted father, pacified him, argued with him. The truth was that she wasn't afraid of him, so he liked her. Gradually she interested him in Italy, her family and friends. She invited people to dinner, and father spoke to them amiably enough. They ignored me, although I sat in mother's place, and I felt unwanted, alone and very stupid.

We had lived like this for six years when Miss B. said one day, "I'm going to a christening party. My friends have asked me to lend them some spoons. Will you lend me yours?" I answered, "Of course." I had twelve little spoons that had belonged to my grandmother and were my only treasures.

"The baby's father is a famous singing teacher," she went on, "and Caruso is going to be the godfather. You can come to the reception if you like." I accepted gratefully and wondered which of my two dresses I would wear—the dark blue serge or the light blue silk. I decided on the light blue silk and a large wine-red hat. I loved my hat.

The guests hadn't come back from the church when I arrived. It was nice to be in a house that smelled of candles and cake. Hired waiters were standing about, whispering, and I waited alone at the top of the stairs. Presently the front door opened and I heard excited laughter and Italian words. A man in a big fur-collared coat came in and the "s" in "Caruso" hissed up at me. He was the first to come up the stairs. He stopped halfway and stood looking at me. In that long instant I knew that I was going to marry him.

Miss B. introduced us in her shrillest manner, in loud Italian. Caruso replied in quiet English. I gathered that she was asking him to dinner. He waited for her to finish, then said to me, "It is at your father's house, *signorina?*" I managed to say, "Yes, Mr. Caruso."

When father heard that Caruso was dining with us he said to Miss B., "Very good thing, very good thing. You may sing in the Metropolitan yet."

On the day of the dinner she spent hours in the kitchen, making special sauces and Neapolitan pastries. Caruso arrived with a great cloak flung across one shoulder and an enormous blue felt hat. He wore a suit of powder blue with velvet lapels, a

44

soft cream silk shirt, flowing Windsor tie, white socks and black patent pumps. (This was his costume in *Julien*. He confided later, "I wore it so you would remember me.")

At dinner he paid no special attention to me but talked chiefly to father, and always in English. A few days afterward he sent us three tickets to hear him in *Aïda*. The seats were in the front row, over the drums.

After that he came to dine often. Miss B. talked and talked about music, and so did father. Enrico listened. He continued to send us opera tickets, always over the drums. Father didn't like this at all, but he didn't say so to Caruso.

Sometimes, on the days when he wasn't singing, Enrico took Miss B. and me motoring. She had explained that I was included only because in his country it wasn't correct for an unmarried woman to drive alone with a man. He sat between us and told us stories of his life—always in English. She listened with a little knowing smile that sickened me.

We came in from driving one February afternoon, after we had known Enrico for nearly three months. Since I was going out again to dine with some old family friends, he offered to drop me off at their house. To my surprise I heard father say, "Very kind of you." Enrico helped me into his car, gave the address to the chauffeur, sat down beside me and said, "Now, Doro, when can we be married?"

* * *

Many times during the months Enrico had been received in our house father said, "I don't see why Caruso likes to come here—he is obviously not in love with Miss B., and he treats you like a child." It never occurred to father that he came to see me.

On the day he called, formally, to ask father's consent I was trembling with fright. I listened to their interview through the

45

hot-air heater that connected my room with the library. After they had greeted each other I heard Enrico say, "I come to ask the hand of your daughter in marriage." There was a pause and father said, "Well, well, well." I think he was too surprised to say no.

Miss B.'s attitude toward me changed from the moment she learned of the engagement. She accused me of knowing that she herself was in love with Caruso and vowed she would find a way to prevent the marriage.

We had taken a house in Spring Lake for the summer, and Enrico often came to spend week ends with us. It was there that I taught him, phonetically, the words of "Over There" from the manuscript George M. Cohan had sent him.

Ever since father had given his consent to our marriage he had welcomed Enrico to the house with warm affection and looked forward to his weekly visits with pleasure. Miss B.'s attitude, when we were all together, was affable; but whenever we were alone she repeated her warning. Then one morning in August I felt a change in father. He showed me a letter from his lawyer furnishing him with information we already knew regarding Enrico's family and fortune. It contained superlative praise for his character and his immense contributions to war charities, and ended with profuse congratulations to father.

"It's wonderful, isn't it?" I cried.

"No, it is not," father said. "It looks very black. He can never again set his foot across the portal of my door!"

I was astounded. Not having any idea of what was in his mind, I wrote Enrico immediately to stay away until I could find out. Father stopped speaking to me and held long conferences with Miss B. in the library.

A week later he sent for me and announced, "I have decided

46

you may marry Caruso after all, but only if he settles half a million dollars on you—and in cash."

In a flash I saw the whole plan. It wasn't a question of money, as father had plenty. Miss B. must have told him that if I married she couldn't remain in the house alone with him because her reputation would be ruined. Father had then tried to find reasons for withdrawing his consent to the marriage and had written his lawyer. This plan had missed fire, but their second plan was surely better: I would never dare ask Enrico for half a million dollars, since I had never dared ask anyone for anything; and even if I did ask him he would be so shocked he would no longer want to marry me.

It was horrible. I decided that there was only one thing to do —meet Enrico in New York, tell him of father's demand and trust to his understanding. I took Miss B. with me to his apartment in the Knickerbocker Hotel, where he was waiting for us. He listened without interrupting while I told him everything. His eyes filled with tenderness and he said, "Doro, you can tell your father 'No.' I have not half a million dollars in cash. I have Liberty bonds but I will not sell them. But even if I had the money I would not give it to you now. After we are married everything I have will be for you—not just half a million. Think tonight what you want to do and tell me tomorrow if you will marry me."

Miss B. and I stayed in New York overnight and early in the morning I telephoned Enrico that I would marry him that day.

My preparations for the wedding were simple—I merely asked a friend to let me charge a dress and hat to her account. The dress was dark blue satin with long white fringes, and the little hat was trimmed with white wings. This was my trousseau.

When I went to join Enrico I found him in his salon, looking

47

at a portrait of his mother. There were tears in his eyes. "I wish she could be here too," he said. She had been dead thirty years and he had loved her very much.

We were married at the Collegiate Unitarian Church on Madison Avenue. Afterward Enrico dictated a letter for Miss B. to take back to father, asking his forgiveness, but I don't know if she ever gave it to him. A short time later, without notifying either my mother or any of his children, father adopted Miss B. as his daughter, thereby satisfying her sense of propriety about remaining in his house. I never saw either of them again. He disinherited us all and when mother died he willed his entire fortune to Miss B.

* * *

All this had happened over a year ago, and now I was married to the greatest singer in the world and in a few months I was going to have a baby. When I first told Enrico about it he said simply, "What God sends we must keep." I hadn't thought much about a baby on the voyage to Italy, or even during the summer, but now I thought: for the first time something is going to happen to me alone—not to Enrico and me, but only to me. It was reality in the midst of heavenly unreality. Three words were to be added to the ending of the Cinderella fairy tale: And so they were married and lived happily ever after—with their baby.

The contrast between my life with father and my life with Enrico was like being transported from the nether regions to the stratosphere—many months had to pass before I could accept even the usual events of Caruso's life as a matter of course. Also, since I was accustomed to father's drastic disciplines, I unconsciously expected Enrico to treat me the same way when something went wrong. But before I had been married a week two

48

things happened which showed me how different indeed my new world was to be.

One hot afternoon I was preparing to take a bath when Enrico called me. I hurried to his studio and he gave me a little gold case, containing my first checkbook with a deposit of five thousand dollars entered on the first page. I was so unpracticed in receiving that I could only say, exactly as I would have said to father if he had given me a dollar, "Thank you, I will try to be very careful and make it last a long, long time." Enrico said quickly, "But, Doro, you must not do that. It is for you to enjoy." Hardly realizing what had happened, I started back to my room in a daze. As I passed through the salon I saw a trickle of water coming toward me from under my bedroom door. "Heavens," I thought, "the bath"! My room was a lake and the bathroom a Niagara. I rushed to turn off the water, then stared in horror at the damage I had caused. There was nothing to be done but confess to Enrico that through my thoughtlessness I had not only ruined an expensive carpet, but also flooded the rooms below— and all this just after he had given me a beautiful gold checkbook and five thousand dollars. Of course he would take them back, be furiously angry and not speak to me for weeks. I sat down with my feet in the water and burst into tears. Presently Enrico came to the door. He stood a moment, looking at my misery, then splashed across the room and kissed me. "No, no, my Doro," he said as I started to speak, "it is nothing. The carpet will be changed and everything put right. Only never look at me again with afraid."

A week later Enrico inaugurated the open-air concerts in Central Park. An escort of motorcycle police accompanied our car to the park, and as I mounted the steps to our seats the mayor presented me with a big bouquet of American Beauty roses, tied with red, white and blue ribbons. I thought, "How

49

angry father will be if he sees me." At once Enrico's voice and the crowd became unreal. I heard again the terrifying sound of father's key in the lock of the front door.

After the concert, when we were having supper at home, Enrico asked, "What has happened to your arms?" They were covered with little wounds where the thorns had pricked me. "The roses," I said, "I was thinking of father." Enrico said, "Someday you will forget the past and not be afraid any more."

* * *

We stopped five days at the Azores to coal. Little men swarmed up the sides of the ship on ladders, carrying baskets of coal on their backs through the heat and black dust.

"Better we go ashore," said Enrico. "I will find a car." The car was a very old open Ford, unpainted and without springs. We drove first to the post office, where Enrico bought all the latest issues of Portuguese stamps for his collection. I was amazed to hear him speaking fluent Portuguese and wondered where he had learned it. "I have often been to Brazil to sing," he said. "But you can't speak Russian just because you sang in St. Petersburg?" "Oh, yes," he answered, "I had many seasons there—plenty of time—it was easy for me." Every day I discovered something new about him—with scarcely a year of schooling he spoke seven languages and had never even mentioned it.

At sea again, on one of the lovely, long, quiet days, I lay on a chaise longue, watching Mario. He wore a gray alpaca jacket and moved quickly about the deck. First he brought out a plain table, leaned on it, shook it—it stood firm. Then he brought a straight chair. He sat down to test it, moved it from side to side— it was steady. Then he placed pens, ink, a ruler and several large sheets of paper on the table. "How is Brunetta?" I asked him. "Very seasick, thank you, *signora*," he beamed.

50

Dressed all in white, comfortable and cool, Enrico came out, smiling happily. He put on a big pair of spectacles that he took from a case marked "*Musica*" and sat down at the table. Mario handed him an old piece of blurred sheet music.

"This is beautiful, this Neapolitan song. It is called '*Tu, che nun chiagne*' ['You who do not cry']. I copy." He measured carefully and drew the bars. The table didn't move. Mario left.

"There," Enrico said at last, "it is finished." He handed it to me. It was perfect—the notes beautifully formed and spaced, all of uniform size and blackness. "How do you do it?" I asked.

"You like, then? When I was a boy—eighteen or nineteen—I wanted to learn to sing, to take lessons, but I had no money. In the day I worked in my father's mill—carried big sacks of flour on my back. That was good work, made me strong but a little tired. I was not paid because I was learning. So to make money I sat on the sidewalk under the street lamp at night and copied songs like this, for the students. They paid me a few lire and I saved them to buy shoes—I had to walk far for my lessons. . . . I will make a beautiful record of this song when we get to New York."

Chapter Two

WE WERE met in New York by Zirato * and Fucito, Enrico's secretary and accompanist, as well as by the usual crowd of reporters and admirers. After our nerve-racking experiences in Italy it was pleasant to be back in a country of contented people and to be driven to the Hotel Knickerbocker by our chauffeur, the devoted Fitzgerald, in a comfortable little green Lancia.

Our apartment was cool, filled with flowers and in perfect order. It was on the ninth floor, overlooking Forty-second Street and Broadway, and the fourteen rooms had been redecorated while we were away. The dining room was on the corner, and next to it, on the Forty-second Street side, were Enrico's studio, dressing room, Zirato's office, Mimmi's room, the pressing room, wardrobe room and Mario's room. On the Broadway side were our bedroom, salon, my dressing room, Enrichetta's room and two new rooms that were waiting for the baby.

Mario, who brought all our luggage through the customs, supervised the complicated unpacking. He turned over the keys of the music trunk to Fucito, those for documents and papers to Zirato, mine to Enrichetta, while he himself took charge of Enrico's. Enrico traveled with his own blankets, sheets and pillow slips, as he could sleep only in linen and, whether in hotels, trains or ships, it had to be changed every day. He had special down pillows and two wedge-shaped mattresses that were

* Bruno Zirato is at present the associate manager of the New York Philharmonic-Symphony Orchestra.

inserted under the usual mattress to prevent all possibility of his falling out of bed. A specially constructed trunk contained our perfumes, toilet waters and all the atomizers, inhalers and medicines necessary for the care of a singer's throat. The first time I saw this mountain of luggage I was appalled.

Mario had a list of the contents of all the trunks, and inside each, pasted on the lid, was a duplicate list. When the trunk lists had been checked they were given to Enrico—a perfect system for preventing loss and confusion. After he had once stated clearly what he wanted done, Enrico never offered advice or found fault; but if his instructions weren't followed, or if they were followed too slowly, his whole manner changed. "Have you a turnip for a head?" he would roar. "Do you think I could sing if I work as you do? Can you stare at the sky and dream and the work do itself? By Bacchus! What are these I have around me— statues?" His displeasure always took the form of explosive and unanswerable questions, after which he would turn his back on the culprits and walk quietly out of the room. His anger was real only when injustice was involved. If someone deliberately used his position with him to further his own ends, or plotted to harm his career, or behaved in a way unworthy of his dignity, then he became cold, scornful and withering. He showed righteous anger when his reputation as an artist was attacked, but lies and calumnies about his private life hurt rather than angered him. He never replied to them—his knowledge of human nature had taught him the futility of denial.

* * *

As Enrico was to sing La Juive for his second performance at the Metropolitan, the music of that score became the background of our days. Fucito came at nine and began to play at once; we could hear the piano faintly as we drank our coffee. Enrico took his coffee black—and so did I. I had never dreamed of black coffee for breakfast before, but after I married all preferences left me. Whatever Enrico ate, I ate; if he didn't eat, neither did I. We were not two people living two lives; we were two people living one life. One and one did not make two; one and one made one, like drops of water meeting.

Every morning Mario brought in the newspapers. Enrico looked at the music criticisms, studied the cartoons and read the news in *La Follia*. At nine, wrapped in an enormous white robe, he went to his dressing room. Mario had prepared the bath with verbena salts and set out the steam inhalator. Enrico did not sing in his bath. After his inhalation, which occupied half an hour, he set a mirror against the window, opened his mouth wide and thrust a little dentist's mirror far down his throat, to examine the reflection of his vocal cords. If he found them too pink he would paint them with a special solution. Dr. Holbrook Curtis always treated his nose and throat, but Enrico himself took care of the Caruso vocal cords.

In the meantime Mario had called the barber. An armchair was placed by the window and beside it a music rack holding the score of *La Juive*. By now Zirato was waiting, notebook and pencil ready for the day's orders. Poor Zirato—I was often sorry for him. He really loved Enrico and tried hard to please him, but he was so anxious that he became overzealous. To overshoot, for Enrico, was as bad as not shooting at all. Unfortunately Zirato adopted a bedside manner when Enrico was nervous. His intention was to calm, but he was so transparent about it that he caused only intense irritation. Enrico interpreted this behavior as a deliberate desire to upset him and said that Zirato was trying to make himself important.

Zirato wasn't a trained secretary. No professional could have held the position for a day, for although he was highly paid he had no time to himself, no regular hours; he had to do anything Enrico asked, and at any time, regardless of his personal feelings. His inexpertness at the typewriter was more than balanced by the speed with which he used two fingers, and his prodigious memory aided the unique method he had invented to keep in order letters, accounts, lists, clippings, albums, collections, engagements, messages and people. He loved music, and Enrico was his god. Toward the god his attitude was either filial, paternal or impersonal, depending upon Enrico's state of nerves. But there were times when he misread the signs and the result was an instantaneous burst of Jehovic wrath before which Zirato bowed silently, sorrowfully. He was the buffer between Enrico and the public; if at times he found the work hard, the rewards were great, and I never heard him protest or complain.

Nearly all famous figures in history have had a trusted factotum—even Robinson Crusoe had his man Friday—and Zirato was as necessary to Enrico after our marriage as before.

After the bath Enrico came in like a Roman emperor, ready to greet his subjects. As the barber shaved him, Fucito played and Enrico followed the score on the music rack, but without beating time or humming. Occasionally he gave orders about engagements, letters and telephone messages to Zirato, who bowed at each order and took rapid notes, murmuring "Si, commendatore."

Meanwhile Mario tiptoed about the room, noiselessly opening drawers and closets. He had to lay out the clothes very carefully; every piece had its place and must be in exactly the same place every day. Enrico sang softly as he dressed, carefully listening to the music from the next room. He was able to dress automatically if his things were in their proper places; if not, his work was interrupted while he called for them. He was demanding, but never capricious.

55

When he was dressed he joined Fucito at the piano in the studio, ready for the real work of the day. He never sang in full voice a role he was studying; he whistled, hummed or sang a phrase on the syllable "ah," explaining to Fucito what he intended to do and what he wanted him to do. Only when he was satisfied with his conception did he use his full voice.

Two hours of intensive work were enough. By this time Zirato had covered the desk with letters to be answered, photographs to be autographed and checks to be signed. Enrico attacked these tasks with the same intensity that he gave to singing. Many of the checks he signed were in answer to appeals for money which he received daily. I never knew him to refuse anyone. Shortly after we were married I said to him, "Surely all these people can't be deserving?"

"You are right, Doro," he replied, "but can you tell me which is and which is not?"

When we wanted a little exercise we drove far up Riverside Drive, then got out and walked while the car followed behind us. If too many people gathered to look at us we got back into the car, drove farther on and then got out again. Sometimes we tried to walk on Fifth Avenue. Enrico liked to "window-shop," but that was difficult because people would stop him and ask to shake hands. We rarely went to public places, theaters or smart restaurants, because the crowds became too great. He never took this attention as a personal tribute. "My face is easy to remember," he said. "But they love you," I said. "No, they have curiosity."

Enrico was warm and cordial, yet in some way unapproachable. Affection was given to him, but he couldn't accept it; there was a vacuum around him in which it could not exist. He didn't want to be stared at and spoken to by strangers whenever he left

56

the house; he wanted to be a private person when he was not singing. He wanted the right to walk in the streets, the right to look in shopwindows, the right to buy one rose instead of a dozen. Often he would say sadly, "Why can't they leave me alone? Why must my life belong to everybody?"

He was powerless against this menace to his peace of mind. Since the quality of his work depended upon his emotional equilibrium, he had found a way to protect his inner life: he put on a mask for the public—laughed, made faces, played the clown, shook the great tassels of the Metropolitan curtain as he took his final bows. He had learned never to take off his mask except when he was at home.

Enrico had no intimate friends, although a group of Italians came to the house every day, each one claiming to be the "closest friend of Caruso" and each intensely jealous of the others. They arrived separately and waited in Zirato's room until Enrico came to speak to them. Often he didn't choose to see them, in which case they picked up their hats and left, united for once in their common disappointment. They were Enrico's entourage, people for whom he cared nothing individually but who, collectively, were necessary to his life. They amused him, spoke Neapolitan with him, accompanied him to lunch when I couldn't go and were self-appointed scouts for art objects to be added to his collections. In return they basked in reflected glory, received free tickets to the opera and huge commissions from the antique dealers. Enrico was completely aware of their motives, but concealed his opinion of them under a mask of jolly goodfellowship. They were harmless, speaking ill only of each other; they spread the legend of Caruso the lighthearted wherever they went. It wasn't until many months later that I realized how dangerous such courtiers could be.

Enrico's greatest friend among the artists at the Metropolitan

57

was the baritone, Antonio Scotti. He lived at the Knickerbocker, in the apartment under ours, and though we didn't see him often we always warmly welcomed him. Before we married he and Enrico lunched together almost daily at a corner table in the restaurant of the hotel and made that corner famous.

Scotti was a bachelor, immensely popular, good-looking and full of charm. One day Enrico came back from his apartment into our salon and poured a handful of diamond, sapphire and emerald rings into my lap. "I give you a present, Doro," he said. As I started to thank him I noticed an apologetic expression on his face. I placed the rings firmly back into his hands and told him to return them to Toto Scotti with the message that although I knew his most recent *affaire de coeur* had ended, nevertheless I was sure his heart would be shortly re-engaged and he would find his rings useful again. Without a word Enrico returned to the apartment below.

* * *

Enrico's nature was not only uncomplicated; it was actually elemental. He was made in large blocks of essentials. His humanity was deep, his humor was broad, his faith was high. He wasn't worn, he was fresh; he didn't need spices. He was able to taste bread—he knew the taste of bread. He didn't have to do anything to sharpen any of the human appetites. The simplicity of his design was too apparent to be readily believed. The public made a mystery of what in reality was a truly simple man.

"Are you a Christian?" he asked me before we married. I told him that I was, and added, "Episcopalian." "I too," he said. "I thought you were Roman Catholic," I said. "I am—and therefore Christian." He didn't know the difference between the different sects of Christianity any more than he knew the difference between our political parties; Christian and American were enough for him.

ANTONIO SCOTTI

Six months after our marriage, when I told him that I had decided to join his Church, he said, "I thought you were already a Christian." It was useless to try to explain, but he was delighted to marry me again at St. Patrick's in New York.

Enrico's sense of humor was that of generations of toilers of the soil. There was nothing subtle about it; it was as obvious as the joy of a peasant at a fair. In winter, when the streets were covered with ice and the wind was blowing a gale, he would stand at the window, looking down on the unfortunate people crossing Times Square, and shout with laughter. "Come quick, Doro," he would call, "see the windy." Gleefully he counted the sailing hats and broken umbrellas and cried warnings through the glass, "Take care, you go now on the slip."

At the circus he was not a spectator but a performer. He joined the troupe from the moment he entered the doors of Madison Square Garden. Avid to see everything, he was as unconscious of attracting attention as a child. He played with the clowns from his box, made faces back at them and, as they left the arena, leaned out to shake their hands. "We make funny together," he whispered. He thought that I and the people around us were laughing at the clowns, never dreaming that it was he who offered us a concentrated three-ring circus. When he visited the freaks it was as if he were calling on friends. "You like to have so many?" he asked the three-legged man in Italian. "He is very funny," he told me, "he say he like because he can kneel and sit at same time." Then he added with pride, "He is Neapolitan, like me."

Although Enrico had no formal education, his instincts were educated. He knew that people's lives would be rich if they would only look into them and not keep looking at the lives of other people. He lived his own life so noiselessly, with such concentration, such intensity, such inner stillness, that he had no need to draw on the lives of others to replenish it. He held his life in his hands, and he was never surprised by it because he gave to it all his attention. Being so full, so rich in himself, he could not absorb the kaleidoscopic life of other people. This is the reason why, when I am asked what Caruso thought of his contemporaries, I cannot answer. He didn't think of them—he greeted them. Only when their orbits crossed his, as on the stage, did he feel their proximity. He didn't speak of them to me except in relation to his work. Even then he neither praised nor criticized their singing; nor did he express a preference for singing with one artist rather than another. His complete absorption in his own work left him neither the time nor the desire to indulge in the usual and useless commentaries on events and people.

Enrico didn't use his sympathetic nervous system for the enjoyment of his art; he used it only to vitalize his remarkable capacity for work. Because he wouldn't vitiate this power, he wasn't able to use his gift for his own enjoyment or for the recreation of others. In this respect he was different from other great artists like Rachmaninoff, Kreisler, John McCormack. They would entertain their friends and themselves for hours, playing with their music as children play with toys. I have heard Rachmaninoff try to sing to John's hilarious accompaniment, and Ernest Schelling play the piano by rolling two oranges over the keys. I have sat in the McCormack living room, listening to these four men explore, excitedly and excitingly, the worlds of art—the discussions always ending with the question: Is singing a creative art? The singer insisted that it was, the pianists that it was not, and the gentle violinist approved the finer points of both arguments. Enrico could not have been drawn into such abstract discussions, since he never speculated or theorized. If questioned he answered only "Yes," "No," or "I don't know." I think he would have been less melancholy had he been able at times to escape from the weight of his music.

Instinctively Enrico avoided parties. When he did accept an invitation, when he had finally decided to go and have a good time, he went not as one anticipating a delightful evening but as one who had already entered a state of pleasure. He beamed at the butler who opened the door, at the footman who took his hat and coat and at all the smiling faces over the banisters as he mounted the stairs. He didn't greet his hostess with charming, untruthful and inconsequential words; he simply said, "So glad," and everyone who heard felt warmed and complimented. He never paid the small polite compliments; he didn't have to—his expectant eyes, his cordial hands, his vigorous back and impelling shoulders pulled and exhilarated the spirit of everyone in the room.

His manner was perfect—at the same time affable and impenetrable. He passed through events and people as if they were a landscape—they pleased him, he pleased them. If he didn't allow people to treat him as a public idol, if at first they were disappointed in finding only a man instead of the god they had expected, they soon forgot their disappointment, for Enrico's gift of making others shine brightly was equal to his own bright light. His stories were robust and not vulgar; his laughter was hearty and not loud. He listened attentively and talked sufficiently. He discussed but didn't argue, and melted away from conversation too heated or too personal. He had invented his own English idiom, and much that was said to him he didn't understand. Because Americans speak quickly and slur whole sentences, he often caught only the last three words of a phrase.

He didn't ask what had been said; he would simply repeat the last three words in a tone of surprise, commiseration or delight, according to the expression on the speaker's face. I have heard him do this again and again, never missing his cue and never being discovered in his trick.

He beamed his way out as he had beamed his way in, and only when he said "Tomorrow I must sing" did I know that he had left the state of pleasure for the state of work.

Enrico lived as he did, not to preserve his voice, but to preserve his life. He restored in his silences the life forces he had expended while singing. The quiet concentrated hours we spent together were as necessary to him as water to a garden. He was a mature and thoughtful man when I married him, and he was entirely aware what the world would say about his having asked a young girl to share a life which, in spite of the public legend, resembled in its deprivations and austerities the imposed privacy of the recluse.

The source of his existence lay only in himself. This was true in every aspect of his life, even his singing. From babyhood he sang as birds sing, without instruction, from his heart; at the age of nine he sang alto in the little church of his parish; for one year, when he was nineteen, he listened to Maestro Vergine teach other young singers. That one year of listening was all the musical training he ever had. The full knowledge of his métier—his musicianship, his technique of voice production, his meticulous standards of quality and nuance, his formalization of his personal emotions—all came from within himself.

Nor did he depend on others to advise, amuse, comfort or inspire him, since he knew that his source was uniquely within himself. He was born with a voice; his perseverance, perceptions, courage and integrity made it a great voice. His knowledge of the

63

nature of his aims accounted for his passion for perfection; his voice was the instrument to be perfected; his consciousness of being his own source was the force which, as in all genius, spurred him toward perfection. Genius is a self-sustaining fire. Whatever may be its mystery, these qualities are surely among its divine constituents.

Everything that Enrico did was as great as his singing because his vital force was expended on each task. As the public didn't know this, they regarded his singing as a huge outgrowth, over-shadowing all else he did. But he always used his full emotional energy for any accomplishment—whether it was for singing a perfect song or making a perfect envelope. Once he needed several large envelopes for his clippings, but had only one. I suggested that we send the chauffeur to fetch more. "No," he said, "I will do myself. That way I learn something new." He took a large sheet of wrapping paper and with the greatest care measured, cut, folded and glued a perfect envelope, using the old one for a model. Patiently he repeated this operation eleven times. When he had finished he shuffled the original model among the eleven others and handed me a dozen envelopes with a smile. "There," he said, "you cannot tell which is it and which is me."

Enrico didn't insist on my living his secluded life. At first I preferred it simply because it was the way he lived; then little by little I realized that I was learning from his wisdom those things which cannot be learned from the outside world. He didn't teach me this wisdom—he exemplified it. He didn't preach tolerance, kindness, generosity, justice, resourcefulness—these requisites of wisdom were the elements of which he was made. He had no superknowledge, but he acted as if he had. His actions were the reflections of his thoughts, and our enclosed life gave me time to think too. We didn't converse about our thoughts. He lived them without words, and I assimilated them silently.

When Enrico cared for people it was for their inner qualities, not for what they could give him. Soon after we were married he told me of his experience in the San Francisco earthquake. After describing it vividly he added, "I save my big picture of President Teddy Roosevelt that he presented me the week before when I sang in the White House. Then I went to London from the earthquake and the King and Queen asked me to tell all about. They were very interested and happy I save the photograph. Such nice people. King Edward so good and so kind." At this moment little old Gravina came into the room. He was an impoverished actor—once a great comedian in Italy—whom Enrico had saved from starvation by making him the cutter of his clippings. One day he had displayed to me an astonishing trick of his comic art—that of shooting his eyes out of his head like a snail—but he was so timid in Enrico's presence that he trembled visibly. When he had left the room Enrico said, "That is a nice kind man too. I like to have him near me." To Enrico there was a similar quality of goodness in the King of England and the old actor, Gravina.

Chapter Three

OUR dining room in the Knickerbocker was large enough for small dinner parties, but when we gave an afternoon reception on New Year's Day, 1919, we took the entire Armenonville floor of the hotel. I was to meet for the first time all the members of the Metropolitan Opera Company and Enrico's friends; he was to meet all my family friends and relations. We sent out a thousand invitations, but three thousand people came.

Enrico and I stood under a bower of roses, shaking hands with everyone and receiving their wishes for happiness. I thought all the strangers were his friends and he thought they were mine. Later we discovered that neither of us knew any of them, but Enrico was glad to see them anyway and made them as welcome as he did the invited guests. A band and orchestra alternated in the two ballrooms; there were lavish buffets of salads and sweets and unlimited vintage champagne. But Enrico and I had nothing to eat or drink because we were still under the bower, shaking hands, at nine o'clock, although the invitations read from four to seven. We were tired and hungry, but since it was impossible to approach the buffets we stole away and ate sandwiches in our rooms. The next day Zirato told us that both strangers and friends had danced until three o'clock in the morning.

* * *

Eleven decorations had been given to Enrico: from Italy, the Order of the Chevalier, the Order of Commendatore, and the

Order of Grande Ufficiale of the Crown of Italy; from Germany, the Order of the Red Eagle of Prussia and the Order of the Crown Eagle of Prussia; from Spain, the Order of St. James of Compostella; from Belgium, the Order of Leopold; from England, the Order of Michael and the Order of British Victoria; from France, the Legion of Honor and the Palm of the Academy.

America as a nation gives no medals for achievement in the arts, yet the honor bestowed on Enrico by the New York Police Force pleased him more than all his foreign decorations. Ten days after our marriage he was asked to sing at the Sheepshead Bay race track on Long Island for the benefit of the New York Police Reserves at their annual exhibition of games and exercises. This was my first public appearance as Enrico's wife, and when we walked to our places one hundred thousand people rose to their feet to applaud, cheer and shout their good wishes. No medal was presented on this occasion, but four months later Police Commissioner Enright came to our apartment and in a little ceremony made Enrico Honorary Captain of the New York Police Force, in token of the esteem in which they held him. As the gold badge was pinned on his coat he asked the Commissioner, "Can I arrest people now?" Mr. Enright said he could. "Then I must go to the Metropolitan right away. I will play a funny on Mr. Gatti."

Enrico's love for America was deeply rooted in his heart. During the four years of the First World War he not only raised twenty-one million dollars by singing at benefits, but gave immense sums to the Allied Relief Organizations and the American Red Cross; he also converted all his prewar securities into United States Government Bonds and invested his income, royalties and salary thereafter only in Liberty Loan Bonds. One day he appeared in the office of "Big Bill" Edwards, the Collector of Internal Revenue for the Second District, and announced that he wanted to make out his income tax in advance and pay it immediately. When Mr. Edwards reminded him that he was anticipating the date of collection by several months, Enrico said, "Thank you, I know. But if I wait something might happen to me, then it would be hard to collect. Now I pay, then if something happen to me the money belongs to the United States, and that is good."

* * *

Enrico had his own art gallery on Fiftieth Street near Fifth Avenue, where he kept his collections of antiques—furniture, velvets, brocades, marbles and bronzes, enamels, tear bottles, snuffboxes and jeweled watches. After we were married he furnished my salon from this gallery. He liked his bronzes best —particularly a certain little lamp. Often after the opera he would open the case, rearrange the figures and hold the little lamp in his hands. "How beautiful it is," he would say. "I love to stroke it softly, softly."

* * *

It wouldn't have been difficult to answer the question, "Why did you marry Caruso?" But nobody asked me that. They asked, "Why did Caruso marry you?" This was slightly tactless, but I was not offended—I myself wondered why. There were many girls much prettier than I, who spoke Italian and knew a great deal about music. I think it must have been my unworldliness that attracted Enrico. In the convent I had been sternly trained in abnegation. We wore plain black uniforms, with our hair brushed back and braided; we sat in silence during meals and listened to a privileged child read aloud from *The Lives of the Saints*. I didn't know whether I was pretty or not, for there were no mirrors and we were closely guarded against such worldly

68

thoughts. If while kneeling in chapel I became lost in a daydream instead of a prayer, a nun would come to touch my shoulder and whisper, "My child, take that independent spirit off your face." I never answered back, never argued. I had been taught the value of silence and attention and humility.

* * *

Enrico didn't like to discuss his singing and as I knew nothing whatever about music he didn't have to listen to silly comments, unasked-for advice and worthless criticism. He never talked shop at home with me. All the business connected with his singing he discussed in the executive offices of the Metropolitan or in his studio. In his letters to me, on the contrary, he often wrote about rehearsals, performances and contracts. As he seemed to wish to keep his life at the theater separate from his life at home, I never questioned him about it, being sure that what he wanted to say he would say. He had no vanity about his voice—in fact, he regarded it almost objectively. Often when talking of his singing he spoke of himself in the third person rather than risk appearing "proud." The magnitude of his humility made an even deeper impression upon me than the splendor of his voice.

His comments about his fellow artists were almost never musical. Once after he had sung a duet with a celebrated soprano, more noted for her beauty than her voice, I asked how he liked her singing. "I don't know," he answered. "I've never heard her." Many of his observations had to do with personal hygiene, since he himself had a fanaticism for cleanliness. If he wore a shirt even for an hour he never put it on again until it had been laundered; in the theater he changed between every act, and had himself sprayed with eau de cologne as he put on each fresh garment. In a certain opera he had to sing an impassioned love song to a large, dark and fat diva while clasping her in his arms.

As he left for the theater before the performance one night he said pathetically, "*Ai me!* It is terrible to sing with one who does not bathe, but to be emotionated over one who breathes garlic is impossible. I hope the public observe not my lack of feeling. Tonight I must act better than I sing."

At another time a French tenor invited us to sit in his box at a concert. Hardly had we seated ourselves before Enrico turned to him and said, "Monsieur, Madame cannot remain unless you go home and brush your teeth." The wretched man left at once, and returned gleaming. Enrico examined him, then said, "Bene, it is important to take care." I didn't understand why the poor tenor wasn't mortally offended and said so to Enrico later. He looked surprised. "On the contrary, he should thank me so to help him. We remained. We might have left."

I can remember only once when Enrico voluntarily chose singing as a subject of conversation. It was when Carpentier, the French prize fighter, unexpectedly called upon us the day he landed in New York to fight Dempsey. Neither of us had ever seen him before. Enrico talked with him for a half-hour, then brought him into the salon to meet me. He was a nice-looking young man and wore an amazing shirt—white with a pattern of large red arrows. "What did you talk about—fighting?" I asked after he had left. "No," said Enrico, "singing." "Does he want to sing?" "No," said Enrico, "he wants to prize-fight." "But you never talk about singing," I said. "Does he know anything about it?" "Well," said Enrico, "he didn't when he came—only to prize-fight. But now, yes." Then he added thoughtfully, "I don't be very much interested in the prize fight."

I loved to hear Enrico sing, but I didn't like opera. To me it was noisy and unnatural and I didn't understand it. I went to the Metropolitan only to see and be with Enrico. Of course I enjoyed all the excitement—I was very pretty, had lovely clothes, and the contrast with my former life in father's house was wonderful.

After we were married I sat in a box for the first time. It was the night after the Armistice and also the opening night of the season. Enrico was singing *La Forza del destino*. I wore white velvet, diamonds and chinchilla. The crowds in the lobby parted as I swept by on the arm of my handsome old uncle; everyone smiled and murmured compliments, and I was in a daze of happiness.

After the second act I went around to Enrico's dressing room. "Do you enjoy, my Doro?" "Oh, yes," I said, "it's perfect. When the lights are on everyone looks at me and when they're off I can look at you." He roared with laughter and then told me that he used to give father seats over the drums for the same reason—so he could look at me.

Two days before, the New York crowds had celebrated the false Armistice. We had been in our dining room in the Knickerbocker, listening to the roar from the street, when Mr. Regan, the hotel manager, came to tell us that the crowd was shouting for Caruso. We went out on the balcony, where two huge flags, American and Italian, had been hung. When the crowds saw Enrico they went mad. He sang the national anthems of America, England, France and Italy; the crowds roared "More!" and he called to them to sing with him. Thousands of voices surged up at us, and Enrico's soared above them all. I asked the florist in the lobby to send us all his flowers and we threw hundreds of red roses, white carnations and blue violets from the balcony. The crowds fought for them and cheered and cheered and cheered.

* * *

Enrico never spoke boastfully of himself as the "greatest tenor in the world." He was more flattered by having a race horse

71

CARUSO AS DON ALVARO IN *La Forza del Destino*
(drawn by Dorothy Caruso)

named for him than by all the eulogies he received on his voice. (He knew nothing whatever about racing, but every day he searched in the racing sheets for news of his namesake, "Enrico Caruso." This horse, whose career he followed with unflagging interest, never won a race; but Enrico placed a bet of ten dollars on him every time he ran.) Enrico could never hear the lovely quality of his voice when he sang—he simply felt something inside when the notes came out well. Only by listening to his records could he hear what others heard. "That is good, it is a beautiful voice," he would say in astonishment. But he always added, a little sadly, "With a beautiful voice it is not hard to reach the top. But to stay there, that is hard."

I realized that it was more than hard—it was a sort of slavery. The more he sang, the more people demanded of him. He could never let down and he drove himself beyond endurance. He no longer sang because he loved it, but because it was something he had to do. And because he was a perfectionist he had no satisfaction within himself; perfect as he tried to be, he knew there was something beyond—a place better than his best. He got no comfort or food from music, but he gave both. I have seen him come home to supper after a magnificent performance and sit, unable to eat, his eyes full of tears. "What is it?" I asked. He held out his palm—"Ashes." It was no use to say, "But it was divine— and you had fifteen curtain calls." It was because of that he wept. And because I understood that these things were beyond words, I said nothing. My silence was a comfort to him.

* * *

We often went to lunch in a little Italian restaurant on Forty-seventh Street. People always recognized him, and he would respond, "Hello, good morning, thank you very much," while Zirato made a passage for us through the crowd. We ate simply in that dark little restaurant—boiled chicken or beef with vegetables, fruit, cheese and coffee. Enrico didn't drink wine. The linen was coarse, the silver dull, the plates were heavy. Pane, the restaurant keeper, served us and his niece did the cooking. He was old and ugly, and, years before, Enrico had helped him when he was in great trouble. But our real reason for going there was because, after lunch, Pane brought out a deck of Italian cards and played with Enrico for hours—no strangers to stare or whisper or speak, just two old friends in an old restaurant, playing with an old deck of cards. I sat with them wrapped in sables, pearls and enchantment

WOODROW WILSON

Chapter Four

O N THE day of a performance there was no music in the house and Enrico rarely spoke. Through the silent hours he played solitaire, drew caricatures, pasted clippings and sorted the collection of rare gold coins he had begun in 1907, when he was singing in Paris at the Théâtre Sarah Bernhardt. He had given me his stamp collection after we were married, and I worked on it across the table from him, as quiet and concentrated as he.

He often said that he would rather draw than sing, and although he had never had drawing lessons he was an expert caricaturist. When he made sketches of himself he didn't look in a mirror; he only felt the contours of his face with his left hand as he drew. A book of his caricatures had been published and every day he made a new sketch for *La Follia*. Years before, Marziale Sisca, the publisher of the paper, had offered him an incredible sum for a daily cartoon, but he had answered, "I do not want money for what I enjoy so much to do. My work is singing—we are friends and I make you caricatures for nothing." Once when we were out walking we saw in the window of an autograph shop a caricature of President Wilson made by Enrico. He waited outside while I went in to inquire the price. When I told him it was seventy-five dollars he was delighted. "That is good pay for work of ten minutes," he said. "Better we stop singing and draw."

He clipped all the war cartoons from the newspapers and pasted them in albums. As his hobby became known, artists sent him their original drawings and people from all over the world contributed to his collection. He was completely happy when he was cutting and pasting, drawing and tabulating. The only occupations that relaxed and amused him were those in which he could use his hands. He cared nothing for books—in fact, he didn't read at all. The only book I ever saw him read was a little worn volume that he kept by his bed. When I asked him what it was he said, "It is a book of facts. You know I didn't have much time to go to school." Years later I happened to look into this book and found written on the flyleaf in Enrico's handwriting a mysterious inscription: "This book was given to me by a man whose tongue had been torn out."

At the end of the silent day that always preceded a Metropolitan appearance, Fucito came and Enrico began a half-hour of exercises. He never sang scales except before a performance. I sat in the studio and listened, watching him walk up and down, a cup of steaming coffee in his hand, as he sang the difficult exercises in full voice. At seven o'clock he left for the theater with Mario and Zirato, and I followed half an hour later.

It has often been stated that Caruso was not nervous when he sang. This is absolutely untrue. He was always extremely nervous and didn't try to conceal it. He himself said: "Of course I am nervous. Each time I sing I feel there is someone waiting to destroy me, and I must fight like a bull to hold my own. The artist who boasts he is never nervous is not an artist—he is a liar or a fool."

* * *

Meticulous about his appearance on the stage, Enrico's make-up was always perfect to the smallest detail and he insisted that each of his period costumes be historically correct.

The make-up for Eleazar in *La Juive* was the most difficult of all his roles, not only because of the heavy eyebrows and flowing beard, but because of the wax nose he had to mold onto his face. It made him frantically nervous. "How can I sing with this

CARUSO AS ELEAZAR IN *La Juive*

thing?" he would shout. "It does not feel well and I tickle from this beard. Give me the scissors—I will cut—I feel very bad." Mario and Zirato rolled their eyes and said nothing. The poor wigmaker and dresser, who had been the targets of this tirade, stepped back and looked relieved when I came in. I put my hands on Enrico's shoulders and smiled at him in the mirror.

77

"Ah, it is you, Doro. Good." At once he became calm and asked for a cigarette, which he smoked slowly in a long black holder, smiling back at my reflection.

When he had finished the cigarette he went to the washstand and filled his mouth with salt water, which he inhaled—or seemed to inhale—into his lungs, then spat out before he strangled. Mario held out a box of Swedish snuff from which he took a pinch to clear his nostrils; then he took a wineglass of whisky, next a glass of charged water and finally a quarter of an apple. Into the pockets that were placed in every costume exactly where his hands dropped, he slipped two little bottles of warm salt water, in case he had to wash his throat on the stage. When all was ready Mario handed him his charms—a twisted coral horn, holy medals and old coins, all linked together on a fat little gold chain. Then came a knock on the door and Viviani, the assistant stage manager, asked, "May we begin, Mr. Caruso?" Just before he left the dressing room he called upon his dead mother for help, since the thought of her gave him courage. No one ever wished him luck because, he said, that was sure to bring disaster.

* * *

Enrico was often asked, "What is your favorite role?" and he always answered that he had none—"Every role is hard work. Of course I like everything I sing. I cannot sing it if I don't like it, and what I don't like I won't sing." He especially loved to sing La Juive because it gave him an opportunity to prove that he was a great actor as well as a great singer. Undoubtedly his most popular role was Canio in Pagliacci. I could never tell to what point he was affected when he sang the famous "Vesti la giubba" unless I was standing in the wings. I have seen him sob for five minutes in his dressing room after the first act; I have seen him fall on the stage, faint from emotion; and I have also seen him

78

come off whistling gaily and joking with the chorus. Whatever his own emotions were, his audience was invariably overwhelmed. I asked him to explain the secret of this power. He said, "I suffer so much in this life, Doro. That is what they feeling when I sing, that is why they cry. People who felt nothing in this life cannot sing. Once I had a great suffering and from it came a new voice. It was in London this thing happen to me. I was alone except for my valet Martino. With this suffering that night I must sing *Pagliacci*. Already I had been singing for many years, but that night was different—I became something more than a good singer that night."

Ten years before this tragedy, when Enrico was twenty-four, he was singing the role of Rodolfo for the first time in Livorno. The soprano Giachetti was making her debut in the same opera. She was also young, and very beautiful. Enrico fell deeply in love with her, and she with him. They couldn't marry for many reasons, but they made a life together. In time a son was born,* and, some years later, another.† Enrico wasn't happy in this relationship, but even after ten years, in spite of many heartaches, he was as much in love with her as ever. He had already sung several seasons in London and had bought a house and garden there for the children and their mother.

He couldn't always be with them. One year he went to sing in South America before the London season opened, and as usual left the devoted Martino in charge of the household. On his return he found only Martino—Giachetti had gone, taking the children with her. She left a note saying that she no longer cared for him, that she would never return. She didn't even tell him where she had gone.

Enrico went mad. He sent telegrams to every city where he thought she might be, but she never answered. His heart broke.

* Fofo. † Mimmi.

Nevertheless, he had to open the London season, and an ironical fate had chosen *Pagliacci* for the first performance. On that night Enrico didn't have to pretend to be Canio—he was in fact the betrayed lover, singing his own tragedy.

KAISER WILHELM II

From that time on he refused all invitations, received no one and stayed alone with his faithful servant, who never left him day or night. Martino ate all his meals with him, walked and talked with him and slept just outside his door.

When the London season finished, Enrico had to go to Germany to sing. As in other years, a few days after his arrival he received a command invitation to dine at Potsdam. No one else was ever invited to these dinners, for the Kaiser wished to talk only about music and to hear Enrico's opinion of the operas to be given during the season. It was almost a business meeting.

"I won't go," Enrico said to Martino, "I don't want to go anywhere. I will say I am sorry." "Signor, you cannot refuse—it is a royal command." "No, Martino, I go nowhere without you." Martino silently handed him pen and paper. "It is true, I must go," said Enrico, "but I will ask a favor of His Majesty. The Kaiser is very stiff, very proud—but music makes him a little different. I will ask if I may bring my servant Martino who is with me always." . . . The Kaiser's answer was "Yes."

The state dinner for two was served in the banquet hall of the palace and presided over by a major-domo who gave all his orders by moving only his eyes. Footmen in imperial livery passed elaborate dishes, and behind Enrico's chair stood Martino, with his little mustache and upturned nose, dressed as usual in a dark blue suit and dotted bow tie. He was unimpressed by the magnificence surrounding him, for he was concerned only with Enrico's appetite. From time to time he leaned a little forward and looked into his plate.

The conversation took its usual form—a series of sharp questions. What new operas would be sung this season? Which had London liked? And Buenos Aires? Enrico answered with proper formal courtesy.

At the end of the dinner the Kaiser raised his glass. "Mr. Caruso, I want you to drink a toast with me." Then for the first time he looked at Martino. "To your servant, Martino—and if I were not Emperor of Germany, I should like to be Martino."

* * *

Enrico read the music critics' reviews with great interest and preserved them in big scrapbooks because they showed him what the public liked about his singing and acting. In one of these old books I came across this criticism, dated December 25, 1914: "Neither Geraldine Farrar nor Enrico Caruso were vocally at their best. Caruso sang with great emotional intensity despite the difficulties he had to contend with in his mezzo voce." Across this notice Enrico had written the word LIAR, in huge letters with exclamation points.

Once his anger against unjust criticism manifested itself in icy calm and immediate action. It was after a performance of *L'Elisir d'amore* and Enrico had felt from the beginning that he "had his audience in his hand." This was exceptional because he always asked me anxiously after a first act, "Do you think it goes all right? Do you think I got them?" But this time he had had no doubts. He was delighted, took dozens of curtain calls and went to bed happy. The next day every criticism was bad. Without a word he went to his desk, wrote a letter and handed it to Zirato. "Take this to Mr. Gatti-Casazza." It was his resignation from the Metropolitan.

Within half an hour Gatti was in the house, frantic. He strode up and down, rubbing his nose, waving his arms. Enrico smoked quietly and watched him. He let him finish his appeals, then said, "No. The critics said I sing badly—but I have never sung better. They know that too. Therefore they are telling me that the public does not like me any more and that the clappings means nothing. So I go away. That is all." Mr. Ziegler also came to add his pleas, and so did Otto Kahn, who was chairman of the board of directors of the Metropolitan. Finally when everyone was exhausted, and poor Gatti weeping, Enrico gave in. "All right. Finish. I sing." In their relief they laughed hysterically, slapped him on the back and thanked him over and over. After

82

GIULIO GATTI-CASAZZA

they had gone, he shrugged. "There! The critics will learn a lesson. Now I am hungry. Let us go to Pane's for a little lunch."

* * *

It was September and our first separation was approaching. Enrico was going to Mexico City for a season of opera and at the highest price ever paid a singer—$15,000 a performance. (At the Metropolitan his fee was $2500. He sang twice a week, and a clause in his contract gave him the privilege of buying fifty tickets for every performance at box-office prices.)

Zirato, Mario and Fucito were to accompany him, but I couldn't go because I was expecting the baby in three months. I was not only miserable at being left behind but worried about Enrico's health. The headaches from which he had suffered so much in the past few years had become even more violent. The year before, I had heard him sing opera after opera while his whole head jerked from the throbbing in his temples. Zirato and Mario knew how to take care of him in these crises, but it was to me he turned as a refuge from fear.

One afternoon when the household was busy with preparations for the journey he came into the salon, sat down beside me and announced, "I have a new servant. I am taking him with me to Mexico."

"Who is he? Do you know him?" I asked anxiously.

"Yes," he said slowly, "yes, I know him. He came to ask for work this morning. I told him if he wish to be the valet of my valet he could stay. I will tell you a story. When I was young, doing my military duty in Naples, I wanted to sing. My sergeant helped me to have an audition with Maestro Vergine. He was a great teacher. He heard me sing and said, 'You have a voice like the wind in the shutters.' I felt very bad, but he had a class of pupils and I asked if I could listen while he taught them. He

84

said yes. He had a daughter who was engaged to his best pupil, a man named Punzo. This Punzo was a proud and stupid man, but the Maestro said that one day he would be the greatest tenor in the world. I spent my free time listening to the lessons. I sat in a corner and no one noticed me. Then my brother took my military duty for me—very kind of him—and I spend more time in the class. My black suit had turned green, so I bought a little bottle of dye and dyed it and pressed it before I went. My stepmother cut my shirt fronts from paper, so I would look nice. I had to walk very far every day to get there—shoes' cost money, so I sang at weddings and funerals to make a little. I remember the first pair of shoes I bought myself—very pretty, but the soles were cardboard. Halfway to the Maestro's house came the rain. My beautiful shoes were wet. I took them off and put them by the stove to dry. They curled up and I walked home on bare feet. At the end of the year the pupils had their examination. When all had finished I asked the Maestro if I could try too. 'What! You still here?' he said, but he let me sing. 'You have no voice,' he said, 'but you have intelligence—you have learned something.' He got me my first little engagement. He was very kind to me when I was young and poor. Punzo married the girl but did not become anything. He is the man who came this morning—and he is still very proud and stupid."

"But why do you want him then?"

"Because I will show him how to be a good valet—then he will know something and not be stupid any more."

* * *

Before Enrico left for Mexico he asked about Mario's wife, Brunetta, for the first time. I told him that I had found work for her at Bendel's. He looked stunned. "Someone belonging to my house working for someone else? It is impossible! I must see

85

Mario." I followed him to the pressing room to hear what he would say.

"What the devil is this? You let Brunetta work outside? Are you crazy? You not know me after all this time? Tell her to leave Bendel's immediately. Tell her she is to work for the *signora*—make things for the baby. Never was anybody stupid like you." Mario stood speechless. At the door Enrico turned. "Take a big room and bath for you both—here in the hotel near to me." Then as he walked away he announced, "And your salary is now twice."

Chapter Five

I N THE early autumn Enrico left for Mexico.

My loneliness was overwhelming—he was my whole world, and I was lost without him. My only comfort was touching things that he had touched. I rearranged his clothes, pasted his photographs into albums, sorted the stamp collection and listened to his records. He told me in one letter to try to be "distracted," so I asked my family to dine and play bridge. But I didn't play with them; I went instead into his bathroom and cried into his big white robe. We telegraphed and wrote to each other every day, sometimes two or three times a day. His headaches were worse and I worried about him all the time. The days passed faster if I kept busy—he had said that one must never be idle. "Find something to do, Doro, it is the only way to be happy." So I trimmed a bed for the baby and embroidered little petticoats and dresses for her. It never occurred to me that I might have a boy. He wanted a girl, so it must be a girl. It was the only thing I could give him that he had never had and that he could not buy.

People always said, "It must be wonderful to be married to the greatest singer in the world." I always answered, "Yes, it is." And it was, but only because he happened to be Enrico. He was the greatest person in the world—and he sang too.

His first letter came from the station by messenger and after that I had one or two every day:

In train going to Mexico after Philadelphia.

September 17th, 1919.

My dearest Doro:

First of all I beg you to forgive me if I will write you with my little machine because the train go on like a devil and it is impossible to write with a fauntain pen. Sometime it seems that the body go away from the legs for the strong and suddenly rolling of the car. We look like people which have dring a baril of whisky!

Sure that you will forgive me I go with my Corona and in my special englisch, with the hope that you will understand me to tell you how I suffred when the train left New York. I felt in myself something which I cannot explain. Everiting around was dark and my heart stop to jomp for a wile. My eyes were closed and my maind was full of you. This was a sens of beatitude and I thought that such a dream will accompagne me until my arrival in Mexico but I make mistake because when we arrived at Manhattan Transfer people rusch in my Drowing-Room and disturb my drimming. But I am still in dream even when people talk and will be a dream for me until I come back.

Now I must leave you with my great sorrow. Dearest my Doro! I love you so and will be devote to you, until I go before the universal judgment. I hold you in my heart.

Your

Rico.

The 4th day in the train going to Mexico City, leaving Laredo.

September 20th 1919

My dear Doro mine, all mine:

Last night in San Antonio I received your sweet telegram which dont let me sleep all night and a little because we change train during the night and gat to gat up early this morning, and a lot because you were near me and I heard in my ear your sweet voice telling me so many lovely and nice frases with your sweet way which I never heard before!

It was a great joy for me that you were near me as I am allways near you with my soul.

This morning very early we arrived in Laredo and from where I telegraphed you after been working for many things and going creazy because Punzo forget the key of the trunk which we bring from Italy and one trunk is missed and I had very moch truble at the Mexican costum house. Fortunately we find a nice girl who revised all trunk and after I explain the matter and seeing that I wont brak the lok of the trunk, she understend and let us go.

This morning when I received the telegram in which you tell me that you cry over my letter; do you understand me then? I assure you that nobody put a word in my letter, and even if I make mistake I dont ask if it is just or not. I wish to know well your lenguage to tell you lots of sweet word but you know that my vocabulary is very smool and, for consequence, I tray all my best to let you know how big and strong is my love for you, my beloved.

I am passing a very misery land; a large and immense field with nobody, and if is somebody, is very poor and sporco e spussolente [dirty and smelly]. Now we beguining to see a profile far away of a large chaine of mountins which, with the reflex of a very nice and blu sky, let me remember my beautiful country. It is very hot and since two days we suffre terribly for that. Hope to find little culler in two or three hours, as the conductor assure.

I will be back soon and I will no more go around the world without you.

It is so warm and I beguining to feel a little bit tired, I thing I will take a little rest.

I close this letter in sending you, my all, my very big love and many, many milliards of kisses.

Beleive me yours forever

Rico.

85 Calle Bucareli, Mexico City.

Monday 22nd Sept. 1919.

My dearest Doro:

Finaly there we are after a very long voyage, and what a voyage! Until the American frontier it was not bad because the road and the confort was sufficiently good, but when we pass the border of the Rio Grande was different. The Pulman car was not bad but the confort very poor—no sufficient water— linen very poor—the food just same. The country interesting from the beginning because savage, but at last day very annoying, allways the same.

We stay a night in Saltillo where we take the escourt of fifty

90

soldiers which accompagne us until here. They say that was only a mesure of precaution, nothing else. I was sure that nothing happen, and nothing happened.

In Saltillo, as I telegraph you, I had a bath and a little supper in one of the best hotel, and at the end, the press of the town came to intervistaire me. I said lots good things, and everybody were glad.

. . . At seven we entered in this big house. Was a house of a politicien of the past government, and mounted in French style but no pictures and no little things. Is a little cold but rada comfy.

Have lots servants and enormous salons, for consequence we have 100 serve us, and lots of space to jomping up and down.

I had a very nice bath and brakfast. We fixed a little the rooms in our way, and then I went out to see the town.

Beautiful avenue, monuments too big for the street, houses like in all South American country, people, if not all, a good portion indias, temperature very warm which affect a little my head. Large movement of veicles, and very large hats and very tait trowsers.

I dont know, my dearest, if you understand me but I go on with my best volonty.

At half past two we had our dinner because we dont eat in the night on account of the temperature. Eccellent food and very home-like. Our cook speeks a little French and seems we will go on in a very nice way.

I thing I talk too much of myself, for consequence, I beguining about you.

First of all, many thanks for the joy that you gave me in sending me a telegram every day and I hope that you will continue because I need to hear you talking to me as I miss you terribly and the day that I will receive a letter from you will be a big joy for me.

What our dear baby doing? * She give you any truble? Hope not! Do, please dearest mine, write me soon and let me know everythings happen to you.

It seems long, long time that I left you, and when I thing to the time that I must pass away from you, I thing I go creazy!

Excuse me, dear, a newspaper man want see me.

Here I am. I was very kind and very polite. My blood pression must be very low because I am very quite and very condiscendent with everybody.

Have the tuner in the other room which, with his "tin-tin" or "Blum-blum," go right in my head and let go away all the toughts.

Better I stop other ways I dont know what I put down.

Your forever

Rico.

85 Calle Bucareli, Mexico City.

22nd Sept. 1919. 11.30 p.m.

My Doro:

You will be surprised in seeing that I write you at such hour but when you know the cause you will say, "Poor my Rico!" I will tell you: After I finisched to write this afternoon I

* Enrico's love and solicitude for the baby began long before she was born.

had more interviews with the newspaper man, and with Mr Rivera, the impresario, until eight. At that time I was very tired and my head give me lots trouble and I ask to go to bed. I take a glass of milk and three aspirin, and after a little wile I beguinning to sleep.

At half past ten I wake up and feeling like I was pinged by somebody. I tourn up the light and looked around and there was nobody. I tought that was my tiredness but there again a ping on my nek. I slap my nek and in retire my hand I saw a spot of blood. Yes, it was blood of bed-bug! I looked around my bed and find three of that ugly bestie! I killed all and went in bed again. I tourne down the light and try to sleep but after a little wile again a ping! I gat up and put all the bed out of place; there, under the matalas were a little nast of such insect! Brrr! I killed all, but my body continue to scratch terribly! Now I see my shirt plenty of spots of blood; it means I killed many of them with my body.

It is very funny for me because I never had such experience, but being accustumated with the cacaroces on board, I thought this was nothing but there was so many and so smell bad that make me stomaketed and scrath for all my own. I dont know what I will do because everybody sleeping, and being so tired, I thing I will pass the rest of the night walking for the room. It was so clen, the bed, and look so confortable when I went in, that I tought I will pass a very confortable night. But here I am, and that will be the six one which I dont have a rest. I dont know what to do. I feel so lonely and here is so cold around me and seems that I am afraid of the noise that the pen doing in writing! I stop for a little wile because I want to scratch myself. Here I am again. I am all red, nearly with the skin broken for the strong scretch! My! My! What you thing that I do? Go to bed again and try to sleep? I thing so! If I will be pinged again I will pass the night here to write to you.

You are now nicely sleeping like a little angel. I am so far. My soul is near you and he kiss you for me.

Goodnight, my treasure
Rico

Calle Bucarelli 85 Mexico City.
26th Sept. 1919. 2 p.m.

My dearest Doro:

What day today! Even your two telegrams was not able to let my pain releieve! It is terrible! I dont know what I can do! I am afraid that something will happen to me because I suffre too much!

Imagine that during the night I had the idea to cut my nek and let go out the blood! I dont know if this pain, so strong, is the effect of the weather, or I am still empoisoned from the train. Never was like that! It is continue the pain in the nek, and nothing is able to let him go.

My life is so reguladed and no reasons to be in so bad conditions. For consequence, if I feel better I will sing; otherwise, no.

When will I see your writing? hope tomorrow.

I love you, my adored Doro, and no more will I be far away from you.

Your

Rico.

94

My only and dearest Doro:

Eureka! Your first letter arrived! What a joy! I am another man since 1 p.m. I am so glad and feeling so much better. Yes, dear, your letter was a balsam for me, and I thank you very, very much.

It was 1 p.m. when I went to the theatre for the first reehersal, that Mr De Rivera told me, "I have something for you that make you feel better." Quigly I told him, "A letter from my dear Doro?" "Yes," he say, and give me your dear message. I kiss many times the letter and put on my heart, which jomping terribly for joy.

Ah, Doro! You dont know how good for me was your writing! In a moment pass before my maind all our life and I saw you in all your movements. I open the letter with fever and reading you with anxiety, without paying any attention to the noise that the orchestra made.

You are lost without me? Immagine what is my condition! You have around you many things that talk to you about me, but I, poor me, have nothing with me, only your picture. But in my heart and in my maind is everything of you. I close my eyes and tink I see you near me. Never more I will go without you in any place! It is terrible! I had a life for the past years, but such life was without interesting, but now—oh, now is different! I am without voice because you are not near me.

What a pity that I dont know your sweet lenguage because I have many affectuese frases to tell you but I cant put down and sometimes I am afraid to write you, I think you laugh at me. Yes. I am afraid because I think that I am not so intelligent for you, and perhaps one day you will leave me! Oh no! You dont do such a terrible thing! I will kill you in a terrible way! You are mine and you will die with me. Do you understand? You dont know me yet, and be afraid of me, because I am terrible in my vengence. Remember that I am geloso, but you never will see me so.

Now we go on to answer your letter.

I am glad that all your family take care of you, and I feel that all belong to me because I like all.

I have sent a postal to our dear mother and hope she is very, very well. If you write to her dont forget to remember me to her, which I love like my dear mother.

. . . At six I came home and lait down for a wile because my head give me terrible pain.

At 8.35 we went to a theatre where all the Mexican operatic artists give a performance in my honor. There was a craudy and when I came out from the auto, a big and long applause broken the quiteness of the street.

We went in a box which was decorated with flowers and flags, and soon I gat in the public gat up, and another applause and urra came.

The performance began with second act of "Rigoletto." No bed. Then came the second act of "Butterfly." Nice. Beautiful voices. After came one act of concert. This was very funny because there was a people who dont know about singing and the

96

public was very severe. Then came the second act of "Aida," and the performance finisched at one.

I came home very tired and went quigly to bad.

You only, you are in my mind and in my heart, and I feel sik because I am far away from you.

Believe me your forever
Rico.

Bucareli 85 City of Mexico
Sept 29th 1919 4 p.m.

My dearest Doro!

Do you forget me in such day? I dont want beleive! It is terribly and horribly and specially after the message which I received last night about ten o'clock. I expect all morning until now another message of good wishes from you but nothing arrived! There was a telegram but was from my jeweler. I thought was from you, and my heart beguinning jomping of joy, but was a disillusion! Bad one! Forget me in such a day! But my heart tell me that before I go at the theatre I will receive a nice telegram from my dear, dear Doro.

As I told you this morning in my telegram, I feel much better and I think tonight will be great sucess.

I was so afraid the past days because my head give me much truble.

Thanks God today I am perfectly well, even that it is reaning. This town is very funny. A moment is perfectly clear and in a

97

moment the clouds are so strong and dark and reaning like a river, then after half an hour, clear again. Such a changeable weather affect me very badly, and on everybody. In effect, Fucito is not well, and I think everyone in the house most pay the tribute; first was Punzo, then Mario, I, and now Fucito. Soon will be the tourn of Zirato. Hope everything will be allright and soon pass this month.

Then, no news of Mimmi? Well, if he write you, you will respond, otherwise, no.

Now I live with the hope that I will receive before my performance a nice message from you; if not, I dont write you any more.

All my love and a thousand kisses.

From your forever

Rico.

On September 29 Enrico made his Mexican debut under the direction of José del Rivera at the Esperanza Iris theater in *L'Elisir d'amore*. He was deeply disappointed that my telegram of good wishes for his success didn't arrive in time.

Mexico City, Bricoreli 86.

September 30th, 1919.

I dont know how beginning this letter!

Can I call you with the usual sweet name or with a bad one? To beginning as the usual must be the usual way of correspondence between me and you.

You broken this usual way! Yes, you let me pass a day (yesterday) and last night in a terrible mood because no news from you. And in such a special day!

I dont sleep all night in thining what happened to you. Lots of bad thoughts pass in my maind about you!

Everybody cable me nicely wishing me a success and you, no! Wy? I dont know what can I think about! It was not foult of transmissission because telegrams arrived to me yesterday from the morning to the night, but yours or one of your family, no! My maind work terribly and I dont arrive to understand how that happened. Are you seek? Hope not! Then what was the cause that I.dont receive a wish from you? I had the intention to not write you until that I will receive your message but I cannot because my heart dont want and this morning very early I sent you a cable asking what about and hope you will answer as soon as possible.

The success last night was plain and tremendous because everybody dont expect what I was capaple to do. At the beginning I was very nervous and the public very excited. You can ear a fly mouving in the sala(room). I sing my first little aria with great emotion and there was few applaudissment. . . . Here Mario bring me three telegram. I will open first one. . . . No! The second one. . . . No! Hope is the third one. . . . Urra! There is your lovely message! Yes, it is the one you sent for the after performance but not the one of wishes which I care immensly. Never mind, I have your message and I know that you are well and now I am glad; even my headeak go away rapidly. Now I can say my dearest Doro. Thank you, and I go on with my performance.

I was very nervous after that little song because I felt that the public was very bed prepared because before the season beginning many newspaper attaccarono the impresa and me in telling that I am old and on the decadence, but when I sing my "largo" in the duet of the first act. . . . What expplosion!! Everybody was creazy and we stop to sing for a while. I got my public from this moment. At the end of the act which I put two top notes very strong and beautifully the entusiam was to the zenit. But my heart! He jomping terrible and nearly I felt down! there was lots of callings to the cortins and lots of congratulation in my dressing room. The second went on nicely and the public was very amused because there was a understanding between. I never heard such noise after my big aria even in the Metropolitan. Do you remember the big noise that the weather makes when we was at home in Italy? That was last night after my "romance." Everybody clapped strongly and "gridavano come dannati" [shrieked like the damned] "Bravo, bravo, bravo!" Heat, hendcaciff, sciarf of men and of women came like banners. For near ten minutes they applauded and call for encore but it was not possible because my condition of nervs was very excited and then we finished the performance nicely. Too bed I was not well accompagned because the other artists were very poor. The press this morning is simple wonderful and I am glad because I have now everybody in my hand.

Now I go to make my toilet because is later and I must go to the reharsel.

> My love,
> Rico.

My dearest Doro:

I have here before me four letter of you dated 20, 21, 22, and 23 September, and I thank you, dear love, very, very much.

You dont immagine the joy which you had give to me with your Italian. It is so kiute and I feel that you are near me and I hear your sweet voice that caresses my ears and makes beating my heart.

But the big surprise and the most big present which I appreciate very much, it is your little foto. I kissed lots, lots times and I hope you will give me a such and pretty girl. What joy will be for us! I think I will be so happy. My soul, I love you so much. Dear, my Doro!

Please dont take any grammatica when you write me because I understand you very much, otherwise you force me to take an inglisch grammere. The only think which we can do, it is to correct each other and I will be the one which beginning to correct you with the hope which you will correct me.

Dont pay any attention to Mimmi. The only think to say to him is this (and you will tell him); if he care for us we will care for him; this is all.

Poor little, adorable dear one! Love and kisses to you and Puschina.

Your

Rico.

On October 2 he sang his second performance, *Un Ballo in Maschera*. In his morning telegram he said that he had rehearsed with the company until after midnight. He had not sung it since April, 1916, in Boston, and since it was a very heavy opera he was more nervous than usual.

Mexico City, Bricoreli 85
Oct. 3rd 1919. 2.35 a.m.

My own Doro;

Dont tell me go to bad because is later. I dont feel to go to bad because I want to talk with you. I know it is later and specialy after performance but I have won duty to accomplished and I dont want to go to bad before to do it. Then, here I am.

I will preceeded by order. After I left you with my last letter I beginning to do my toilet and after I went to the theatre This was crowded. The opera, as I told you in my cable, was "Ballo in maschera." I was little nervous because no message from you, but I excuse you because I know that you dont know when I sing.

My soul was a little troubled. Many thinks happened and the rappresentozion should not be of the best. The soprano, very poor. Papi refused to condoct, for consequence you will understand wath was my feeling to go to sing after lots of sufference which I suffered all day on account of my headheak.

I arrived at the theatre 8 p.m., make me up and dressing in short time and at 8.45 the performance beginning. My first song was applauded but I remark that the public was prevented in a bed way. The first act finished with two cortins calling.

CARUSO AS RICCARDO IN *Un Ballo in Maschera*

The second act beginning well because Madame Besannzoni, the one that we met at Pane restaurant, as a beautiful voice. Then came a trio with me and the soprano. That soprano have a poor voice, with a tremulo and the public dont like. Then we sing a trio and no succes. After come my barcarola and in the first part of that I took the public by the nose and there was a scoppio (burst) of applause. I make a sign with my hand in saying, "It is not finisched." Then I sing the second part and at the end the succes was complet. The "Scherzo ad é follia" was sing very well but the public dont understand. The third act I have a duet with the soprano and a trio with the baritone. This two pieces was and was not a succes because this two people knows only the romances and the rest nothing. If I was the public I do the same thing wath the public doet. Tch! tch! tch! In the forth act I have no part but here dont make any intermission from the first and second part as I am accostumated. Then after the first part of the 4th act finished they beginning the second part without tell me anything. But I heard my music and jomping from my dressing to the stage like a bomb. The public understand and being the orchestra repited two times the music, I was in time to attack my song. There I have a good frase and the public was creazy. The finale was excellent and at the end of the opera I was obliged to go out all alone three times. Everything finisced in a good way but the soprano was a very disastre.

Excuse me I go to bed, and let me sleeping.

I love you,
Rico.

On October 5 he gave an open-air performance of Carmen in El Toreo—the first time he had ever sung in a bull ring—before 22,000 spectators.

Mexico City, Bricoreli 85.
Monday, Oct. 6th, 1919. 7 p.m.

My dearest Doro:

Only now I have the possibility to take the penn and write you. Hope you are not ungry with me because I must be short otherwise this letter not go away tomorrow morning. Then I begin from yesterday and precisely from the moment which I left you.

After I make all my preparatifs I went to the Plaza. This is the arena of bull fights, with now a stage in open air for the opera. There was a beautiful sunshine, but my voice was like midnight, dark very dark, and I was trembling. I dress quigly and put some things in my throat and ready for the performance. At half past three exactly we begin and I went out. An applause salut me but not enthusiasticaly. I beginning to sing and the voice was very strong and eavy, but I quigly juge myself and tought that I go well to the end. Then come the duo with Michaela, poor, very poor, and at the end of the duo, being nervous, because the Michaela not go well, my voice dont sound well but pass, and the public applauded. From that time the weather beginning to change and big clouds beginning to gat up, in effect, before that the first act finished, beginning to reinning and I and Carmen were all wet. We supposed that the public goes away but nobody move. At the end of the act we have few calls. The second act beginning with eavy reinin and there were big spectale. Thousand

CARUSO AS DON JOSÉ IN *Carmen*

of umbrellas was open and covered all the aera of the Plaza. We dont see any head and dont hear the orchestra. We hope allways to stop but the public was there. I begin to sing my romanza and at the midle I dont now if was effect of the rein on my condition, I think that was the reason, one note come out broken. Quigly I tought, "Now come the revolution," but nobody say enyting and I went to the end with more calor and entusiam and the public make me a big ovation. But there the rein that come down strongly. We finished the act and had five callings. It was very funny to see one enorms bleek spot all around the Plaza with some color reed and bleu, there were all umbrellas.

The third act was worst and we went on just same, but at the end was insopportable. I ask, "When we stop?" Somebody told me, "When the public say stop." But nobody told this word. I had a big ovation at the end of this act being in good condition as my voice warmed up. Somebody had the bed idea to say to the public that the performance was finisched because the artists dont want sing eny more on account of the weather. I was in my dressing room to prepare myself for the last act and I heard a big noise. You most know that our dressing room are under the stears of the Plaza and precisely where the bulls are prepered. Then I heard this noise and it seemed like a revolution. I sent out to see wath was the matter and they inform me wath happened. Quigly I sed to tell to the public that the performance will continue. In effect, everybody whent at place because they beginning to broke the stage. Then we finisch the opera with a big pouring and half of the public which dont hear enytinks because the noise of the wather was strong on the umbrellas. We were all wetted and the succes was only for that because artisticali we were all bed.

This morning the press was not bed, only one newspaper talk about my misfortune but in a good way.

. . . Some people come to take me to a place calling the "Little Venice"—about forty people, men and women. I was a little annoyed by the acting of Fucito and Zirato because they looks like they never had see women before. This heurt me because I dont like that the people thinks bed about they, and for consequence about me because they are at my service. The people never mesure herself. In effect, I am showing to both and never more I will bring bak with me in any amousement.

Good night, dear sweetheart, and at tomorrow.

With all my soul I send my love,
Rico.

Mexico City
Oct. 7, 1919. 6 p.m.

My sweet Doro:

Then, sweetheart, you cry on my letter? Wy? Have I the power with my bed englisch to let you cry? I dont want that your beautiful eyes cry. I want that you laugh when you are alone but I like that you cry near me to that I can help. You must dont cry even for funny and I never will let you cry. You must enjoy of your life and of my love.

Now some news of my life. This morning I pay the first bill here, $1860.00 for near two weeks. I tink this is to much but I must pay. Imagine, I pay the bill of the towel and the matresses, and the rent of the house for two months. Such expence was because this house where onfornisched and being so big, we needed for many tings. When I go away I will send all the tings which are impossible to carry with me, to the hospital.

At 2 p.m. we went outside of the town for lunch. There was Mr Trepiedi who invited us, but this man must be called "Onepiedi", because he is short of intelligence. He say that the lunch will be "en famille" but there was many people of the Italian colony, beginning from the Ministre. That was nothing. The dinner was fine. At the end Mr Trepiedi come up and make speek and say, "I must thank Commendatore Caruso and the Ministre for the honor which they had to come to my house." I was making a sketch and I heard what he says, and with laughing, I sad, "Here, here! The honor is yours." Everybody laughing. He sad, "Excuse me, I have a little cognac in my head and made mistake." It very funny until here. But he continue and invited me to remember that the Italian colony is poor, and ask if I will sing for the poor. This was the point of the lunch. I stopped to sketch and told few words in thanking, and let remark that it was not necessaire to give me such a Lucullian dinner which was better to give to the poors, and showing himself how to be charitable. But all this was telling with laughing, but the concret was that I dont need a lunch to make a charity. I dont know how the presents took my words but there was a silence like when the people make a "gaf." All the world is the same!

Then goodnight, treasure of my soul, and love me as much as I love you, much, much.

Always yours
Rico.

My own and sweet Doro:

This morning soon I wake up I asked if there were letter for me. The answer was, "Sorry, not one." My face became blak and I swear against the bandits which blow up the train last week, because I tought that all your letters were burned in the fire of the train but I put my soul in peace and said to myself, "You must wait for."

After that I beguinning to think how many days I will be without your letters and my mind works very, very hard. "Of course," I say to myself, "There is the telegraph," but is not the same thing, because in a cable we feel allways the cold or the heat of the hands of the employees who transcrive the messages.

At one p.m. I went to the barber to cot my hair and manicure my unghie [nails] because both were very long, and at three I came bak. We had our lunch and after, Zirato like a creazy, sleap his face, and says to me, "Commendatore, forgive me! I am a beest! I beg you to pardon me!" and he put the hend in his pocket and took out four of your letters which arrived when I was out. Immagine my joy! Thanks, dear!

No, my Doro, it is impossible that you love me more than I do. You are young and dont know enough of the life and love. I gat you in a time which my heart was push down by circumstance of the life but, being catched by you and free of the heavyest, he push out all his power of the love on you, I means he push out all the poison which from many years was in it, and put in his new love which is rappresanting from my own and sweet Doro.

Then, I say that it is impossible that you love me more than I do, and one day we will see who is right. Doro, Doro, I adore you!

Glad to know good news of Mimmi, and I hope too that he will become a really man.

Thank you, dear, for the silk pads you put in my bureau drawers, and sure I will appreciate very much.

Tell to the baby to be quite. This is the veritable joy, and I thanks God for such happiness.

Then good night, my adorable little wife, and with a tender and affectuose embrace.

Believe me your and always
Rico.

Mexico City Bucareli 85
Oct 9th, 1919. 3:30 p.m.

My sweet Doro:

Last night at the rehearsal I cant put out any sound, and this morning before beguinning my toilette I looked at the vocal cords, and they were very red. You can immagine my state of nervousity! Then I went on with my toilette and after the bath I went in bed again and sleep, jomping, until 12 o'clock. I called Mario to know time because I have no watch, being broken, and he told me, then he give me two letters of you and I put them on my heart. I reed them three time and I gat up. I looked my throat again to see if the medication which I make myself was effective. Yes, the cords were little better. Then I dress up and went out for walk being a very beautiful day.

My Doro!! What is "a splinter in your eye"? Something hurt your dear eye? "Steel in your pupil"? How that arrived? My poor Sweet! She suffred and I was not there! I am glad that everythings went alright, and I breathe better now.

I understand now why you ask me to pay something to Joseph's. Better you wait for me because I will put all the moncy altogether and will divide to the creditors. I never will tell you anything if you are good or bad, but let you to see things and understand the position which we are. For consequence, I have nothing to say about your expences. I wish to see you always glad and happy, and if one day I have no more money I will work very hardly at pier * to let you enjoy of the life.

I am yours, soul and body. All my kisses and my love for my adored Doro.

Rico.

Samson et Dalila was his fourth performance, again at the Esperanzo Iris theater.

Mexico City,
Oct 10, 1919. 4 p.m.

My dearest Doro:

When I left you yesterday I beginning to try my voice. What a voice, dear! all the centre broken. But little by little I fixed up and with nervs until my hair, I went to the theatre. There more preparatifs, and at the time I went out. The first song was alright but when Samson try to convince the people, my center beginning to be tired. Instead to force the voice

* He means he will do any kind of labor, even to being a stevedore.

112

CARUSO AS SAMSON IN *Samson and Delilah*

I went very careful on the top note and the first scene pass but without any applause. Then came the trio. Was allright. At the second act the voice was warmed up and the duo went on wonderfully. The scene of the mill-stone alright and so the last scene. When I put down the coloms I thank God. There was not enthusiam at open scene from the public but at the end of each act we had five or six calls. Being put lots of things in my throat today I nearly cant talk.

I told you in my cable that I will keep the money because I am afraid, perhaps not, that I will not finisch the performance and for consequence I must give bak the advance. You know I have always bed ideas and sometimes I dont make mistake.

I thank you, dearest, that you find time to write me every days. Yes, dear, when people born square you cannot make him round. I am very sorry for, but better thet your friend let do something to his wife, otherwise their life will be short. Of course his wife must understand that the husband works and he must have the privilege to command. Dont give any advise because we say, "Between husband and wife dont put the finger." Even for your other friend you must take care, because if she is in terrible love with the Capitano, nobody can do anything.

Goodnight, my own love, my sweet and darling.

Rico.

My sweet Doro:

As ever I beginning to write you from the moment which I left you with my letter because it is more easy for me and at same time you know exactly what I doo during the day and night.

There should be a rehearsal of "Martha" but at the last moment a telephone call advice me that there were no rehearsal but, if I dont mind, to stay home to ear a lady sing. And, in effect, at half past eight, Papi, the impresario, and some other gentlemens came with a jung lady. As you know we have not a good soprano in the company, the impresario goes around to find some to repair the loss. She, then sung and the voice were not bed. When I say that she were good the impresario told me that she will sing with me in "Manon" of Puccini. I dont care because I dont want any trouble. At ten oclock I went to bad and all my thoughts were of you. I called you many, many times with sweet names but nobody answer me, and in saying, "Doro, my Doro," I beginning to sleep. Ah, dear, you dont imagine how I want to come home. It seams that I am here from a tousand years and every moment I count the days that must pass.

Am I lonely for my Doro? I whish to die (for funny) and let the Mexican sent away my body to you, then you find me in life and never more go way from you. Oh, sweetheart, you dont know how I love you. It is too soon for you to see how big is my love for you. Lather you will see and you will love me in the same way. My heart jomping so strong, I think he want to fly to you. never more, never more I will leave you. When I came bak I will bring you to a plumber and let him put a ring which will enchain your leg at mine.

I think, dear, with my suffering, I must stop to work and go bak to my country, in a hot place. Otherwise I will go down like a fruit that goes down from the tree. I am afraid to leave you, to die, and I want, yes, I want to stay near you longer, longer to enjoy of your charm and your sweetness.

Mimmi with a voice? I dont think. Glad to know that people like him, and I hope that he will not be spoiled.

Now with sorrow, I must leave you because I must laight down.

All my love, embraces and sweet kisses from your own

Rico.

On October 12 he sang *Un Ballo in maschera* in the bull ring during a violent thunderstorm.

Mexico City,
Oct. 12th, 1919. 6 p.m.

My sweet Doro:

Here I am after a terrible day and I will explain to you but I must beginning as ever from the moment which I left you.

Then, at 3.30 the performance beginning. The voice was fine and my spirit very high but there were some black clouds that beginning to come up, and at the end of the first act, beginning to rein, thin, thin. We beginning the second act, and the succes was great even as in the first act. I sing this two acts wonderfully and everybody were glad and enjoy very much. But in the second act when I sing the barcarola in which the words saying, "io sfido i venti, i lampi, i tuoni ecc" [I defy the winds, the lightning, the thunder] there were a really wind, laight and tonder. Which finish the clouds open and wather came down as a storm. I went in my dressing room to be ready for the third act, and I was ready, when the wather beginning to come down in my dressing room. We stay like that for half an hour and the public was there with umbrellas and overcoats on the head. When I saw that was impossible to stay in the dressing room, I went out and put on a mantel and ask to the rest of the public which were in the box, "Watte we go to do?" They answer me, "Go home." Soon I undress under the reining which come down in the dressing room and come home.

I think it is the first time in my artistic carrier that I bring home some money without work.

What you think if I give half of my check to the poors? I dont feel to take such money but the impresario dont give bak to the public anything. Then I dont see why I must give my money to the poors. I think I will send to my poors relatives.

Tutto tuo,

Rico.

Mexico City Bucareli 85
October 14th 1919 4 pm

My Doro darling:

Here I am with all myself to you. Now I beguinning tell you what passed from the moment which I left you
yesterday . . .

At ten o'clock, then, I went to bed. The pain were there but
not too strong. I try to go asleep soon and I gat it but at half past
elelven I wake up and there were a noise. It was Zirato who
thought I was awake because I forgot to put down the light, and
he gave me two telegrams of you. Before I opened it, I heard
your sweet voice saying, "Rico-Rico, here I am!" I looked around
and of course nobady were there, only Zirato more high then
ever, looking for an answer. Then I put your dearest message on
my heart, after been reading three or four times, and I beguinning
to sleep again. At two o'clock I wake up, and your message was
near my lips! I kissed many times.

Glad like Easter, I gat up and went to the barber to have a
massage. There everybody steel talking of "Martha" performance.
It seems that with this opera I make everybody creazy.

Like yourself I feel to write you every minute, and when people dont let me do what I want, I go crazy and become blek, until
I take the pen and beguinning "My sweet Doro." Then my face
change expression and I become sweet and calm.

I receive a letter from Mimmi, not ver expansive. I will answer
him in the same way.

Now I must leave you with my great sorrow. I will answer tomorrow to your sweet letter of the seventh. Dearest my Doro! I love you so.

I hold you in my heart.

Your
Rico.

Mexico City Bucareli 85
October 16th 1919 7:30 pm

My dearest Doro:

I just came out of the bed because I had a very bad attack two hours ago! Ah! Doro mia! I dont know what I can do for such things! I am so afraid! I dont want stay anymore in this country. I want die with you! I cry because I suffre so and I let you suffre! I dont do anythings bad, then why must I suffre this infernal pains? I am here with short breath and pale like a die people. Two times today I was attacked by this horrible misfortune.

People say God were good with me! I put down my head and supporte His goodness . . .

I wish to have you near me to see your sweet, beautiful face. Doro mia, I adore you better that I adore my God!

Your
Rico.

My dearest Doro:

. . . After I'had read your letters I felt better, and Mr Stefanini told me, "Oh, dear! You forget you have an appointment to go to the bull fight." "Yes, I remember," I answer, "But I must go and write to my dear and sweet little wife. For consequence," I said, "I dont go." But there were a little fight between us, and he convinced me in saying that was very bad to go in my room, closed, and work with my mind, I can do that later.

I thought he was right and went to the bull-fight. What impression, dear! I dont tell you because you will be disgusted like I was, and I think this was the reason of the third attack in the same day. I left before the end because beguinning to feel bad, and come home. But in what conditions! Very bad, dear! No asperine, no electric pad, no other pastils for the case releived me soon! Two hours of sufference! But when I felt that I can move my neck, I gat up and sitting here thinking that if I write you I will feel better and, in effect, now I feel better.

Can I find the words to answre to such lovely and sweet letters? I am afraid, but I put down everything that my heart feeling. All your expressions about me, dearest, make me more of love for you. I never heard such beautiful and sweet expressions in my life and I am very, very sorry to not be able to say to you more, more and more nice and sweet words! I, in lessing * so, do facts, and this not because you are pretty and nice, no, because I love you, and I loved you since I meet you the first time.

Ah! Doro Mia! I love you terribly! I cannot say how I am

* He meant: I, lacking English words, express myself instead in acts.

jalous of you! My jalosy is so big that it make me mad! Some-times I am very cold. Is because my jalosy works inside of me and I dont want make a scene because I dont want make you suffre! My darling! For nothing in the world I will let you suffre and I beg you pardon if sometime I was a little excited but it was because I love you so.

Keep the annonymous letter and dont pay any attention to any one.

Ah! This old man of your father is crazy! I am sorry for him and I hope one day he will become in himself and ask for all his family.

A world of love.

Your forever
Rico.

His sixth performance was *Martha*, at the Esperanza, on Octo-ber 17.

Mexico City,
Saturday October 18th, 1919. 5 p.m.

My dearest Doro and sweet:

. . . I went to the theatre in a very bed conditions. There I tried my voice and I was surprised of the lightness. Then I was a little quite with my nervs but the head-ache were there in bak of my head. The performance beginned and from my dressing room I heard how the first scene goes. Nobody knowed the part. You must remember that I was not at general rehearsal, for consequence the performance were my last prova [rehersal]. I heard that the soprano and the mezzo makes lots of fault and that makes me nervos because I tought at my duets, terzetti e quartetti. [trios and quartetts]

The second scene, the market, beginned and the corus went out of kee and the public show his malcontento in wissly terribly. I went out with the baritono and he beginned with a very wrotten voice. The public were indulgent because this man was an old artist. I beginning my larghetto and with my surprise my voice were without brillancy but my experience let the public applaude at the end of my solo very much and on the ensemble were many applaudissment. But I was not satisfied. We had four courtins calls.

We beginning the second act and until the notturno [nocturne] there were many fault and out kee and situations. Imagine the Martha had no flowers, then, ten messures before I remarked and told her. She dont onderstand. Then I saw that she had flowers on her hat and in singing I told her to take one. Nothing! Then at the moment at which I must take the flower from her corset, I took the flower from her hat and the public laugh. After the song, "The last rose of summer," we have the most interesting part of the duet, and in a moment which nobody expected, there were "Nancy" and "Plunquet." With a presence of spirit I changed the words and instead to sing to Martha, I let understand to this people that was too early to come out. They went away with gesticulation. We continue the duo which was very much applauded. The public call me many times but I went in my dressing room. I came out for the notturno. When I say, "Dormi pur ma il mio riposo" ecc. and I sung that song with all my soul and everybody were emotionated. At the end of the act 6 calls.

There comes the third act were is the romance. Ah, dearie, I dont know where I found such a voice! I never sing that aria so beautifully and there were a demonstration delirante. Twenty minutes of callings and the people were crazy. They call for the encore but dont do it.

After comes the concertato where I have the famous frase, "Marta a te perdonne Iddio." I sung such frase with many feelings and intensity, that everybody public and artists cry, and both applauded with enthusiam. After many callings my dressing room were assalted from all the friends whom I meet here. I saw one trembling so hard that we were obliged to help him. Everybody had tiers in the eyes and all kiss my hands.

The emotions were so great in everybody that was explenid as I never sung in my life like that and I communicated to the public all my feeling with a voice over uman. That was because my Doro was praying for me at that time. I tought then to send you a message and before to every I dictated the cable to Zirato who beginning to cry when I said, "Even with head ache I sing fine." He were emotionated for the succes and for my suffering. Poor boy! I carress his head because he were on his nees, and he says, "Forgive me. The emotion is too strong!" Then he went to send you the message.

The last act was allright and we had many callings.

At moment wich I went in the auto there were a crowd and everybody shake hand with me and some lady kiss me.

We came home and had a little supper and went in bed. I beginning to sleep with your name on my leeps.

Goodnight and at tomorrow.

Always your own

Rico.

123

Mexico City,
Sunday Oct. 19th 1919. 1 p.m.

My dearest Doro:

Am in bed suffering since last night when I left you. All night sweetheart, the pain bothre me and this morning I tought to go crazy. It is now three days that I am suffering terribly and nothing is good to releive me. I am burned for all over my body but this dont do me any good. Imagine in what spirit I will go in two hours to sing "Samson"! No breath, a ball in the stomach, all the nervs from the nose to the neck are attacked. On top of the head I feel if there were a continue laightning. My eyes are swolled and very eavy. Bed umor and no volonty to do enything. Here my head goes up and down like a bell and all the nervs inside hurt me. Ah, my God! what have I doit? Certainly it is a penalty.

I dont want boder you anymore with my pains. It is not pleasant to have a seek man around.

Eternity with you!

Your own
Rico.

On October 19 he sang *Samson* at the Toreo. He was feeling very badly and in his telegram he told me that when he went to the arena he "prayed so hardly for a storm but the sky was very clean." He said he put some balsam of Bengué in his nose and all over his head and neck, and without trying his voice, went out to sing. To his great surprise, he said, "everything went alright to the end."

124

Mexico City Bucareli 85
Monday Oct. 20th, 1919. 4 p.m.

My Doro darling:

Here I am with all my self to you. I count days every instants but never pass. Father Time forgot us. Three weeks more and I will be with you forever.

. . . Your message releived me instantanely. I went abstairs and had a nice hot bath and nice dinner made by Punzo. There were a good consomme, spaghetti with butter, and nice baby lemb. We had the impresario and Delila at dinner with us. They invited erself and sintomatically this means they have something to ask me, and in effect, they want me to sing in a concert next week. They dont said for what occasion will be this concert and I answered evasively.

What about our baby Puschina? Are she good? She trouble you? Do you find the name? What you think about Fiora, Flora, or Florinda? Do you like Erminlinda? Or Floriana? We have time to find some other names if you dont like all that.

Now I leave you because some people is down stairs.

Tender embraces

Tuo

Rico

Mexico City Bucareli 85
Oct 21st 1919 8 p.m.

My own Doro:

Here I am from the moment which I left you yesterday.

I gat up, make my toilette and went out for walk.

I find people, two gentlemen, who were in auto and with force tooked me and went for draive. At twelve I went to the barber and at two home for lunch.

Here we were eight at the table, four we, and four gentlemen whom invited me to go to see a tabac factory. We went at four p.m. and there were kind of business—advertising. I let understand that such business was not proply and, in laughing, I told that for such advertising people pay lots money. If they were Mexican dont said anything, but being French I let them understood that such business were not right. Then we went to see the Theatre National which is a great monument made by an Italian but not complited, and there we loose lots time becuse we sees all the machinery in function.

At eight I came back and find your message. Why you did no say "kisses"?

I love you so, dearest. Here a kiss.

Until tomorrow. Goodnight.

Your
Rico.

My own and sweet Doro:

Have a proverb who say, "The good day beguinning from the morning" and the same at reverse, the morning beguinning bad and finish bad.

Then we arrived at the theatre at half past nine, and there were a box all decorated of flowers. The spectacle beguinning and at the climax of the success for the artist for whom the benefit were given, she thanks to the public and says to salut the great artist, Caruso. There was a tremendous applause and a flash-light. I was obliged to gat up and thank the public. We stay there until half past eleven and came home. Of course I dont amused for nothing, because was nothing interesting, not musically nor artistically. Stupid things, bad voices and Spanish ordinary dances. I suffred so for two things. First for my pain in the head and second that I loose lots of time that I can spare for you. If you were there sure you will annoy yourself like me.

At two p.m. I went to the theatre for the only rehersal of Pagliacci. At four, home for dinner. There was a gentleman, (judge of the tribunal charged to write an article on me) We had a dinner and talking. At five I went to the house of the associate of Mr Stefanini to hear his sister sing and give my opinion. There was a scene because I said the truth about the voice of the girl, and she beguinning to cry hardly and embaraced me and all the present very much. I dont know how I gat out of the situation but I gat. Immagine! She want that I sing one night for her, to pay the expences for study. I had nearly a fight with her brother when we was out and he laughing on my face and told me, "Ah! Mr Caruso, you dont know how much I am obliged to you." I dont understood. He continue, "You have saved me and the girl because she thought she was great, and trouble from morning in the night." We all laughing and came home.

Here I find your two messages about anomimous letters, which make me terribly angry with the son of dog that truble our happiness. I went on fury. There must be the same person who sent the others before.

People take advance of innocence things to hurt us, and think that we go engry. Not at all. We must enjoy to know how many enimys we have and this let us know that people are jalous of our happiness and position. Of course the first impression are bad, but if we consider well why the people do that, we must be proud and laughing on it.

Yes, dear. The little one cost more than a big one because they need more than us. Nevermind, dont think of the expense of our dear Puschina who came to enchaine us for all our life. She will be our delice and increase our happiness.

Your letters dearest, are very interesting and so sweet. I like them very, very much. You are adorable in your mistakes. You are in the same conditions of your Rico. He doesn't know the English but he try to let himself understood. Do you understand him? Yes? Then he understand you. You know why? Because we are made one for the other.

Every baby to the eyes of his mother is beautiful and you will see that for us our baby will be the same, but for the others will be ogly.

If I miss my wife! Oh! Adorable creature.

All sweetness, all caresses, all tendresses and all my love.

Rico

Mexico City Bucareli 85
Oct 23rd 1919 5 p.m.

My dearest Doro:

When I reed you my heart jomp strongly and it seams that he want goes out to tell you how much he loves you. He is so closed up that he cant but I feel him cry and go sad.

You are a very darling with all your expressions and be sure that I will do my best to let have a paradise during all my life.

Mimmi wrote me, but without any affections—so cold. This hirt me very much.

I must leave you with my sorrow but I must do something for my head.

I will cable you little later. A proposito, do you know how much I payed for cables to you? Thousand pesos, that means five hundred dollars, and from your part the same, that means one thousand dollars, both. Somebody else will say, "Extravagant!" but I dont care. How many thousand I am willing to pay if was possible to be near you in this minute.

You know what I doit to be nearly you before the time? I order a sleeping-car which bring me directly from Laredo to New York without stopping any place, otherwise will take one day more.

My love to you, sweetheart, and millions of sweet kisses.

Rico

He sang *Pagliacci* at the Esperanza on October 23.

CARUSO AS CANIO IN *Pagliacci*

My daerest Doro:

I am so sorry for not been writing to you yesterday! I will then beginning from the performance of. "Pagliacci." At 8 p.m. I went out of my automobile at theatre door and I saw all the facade of the theatre decorated with flowers. I went in from the stage entrance and as soon I got in I saw a movement of people and when I cross the stage to go in my dressing room there were four lines of employees of the theatre which salut me with a big applause. The anti-door of my dressing room and this one were all decorated with my picture and palms and flowers. The anti-door ordinarily is a place where all the stage people put all the material. That night there was like a parlor to receive a king. Flags, palms, flowers, picture and lots different plants all around makes the ambiente very pittoresque. Everybody smile and clapped and said, "Viva il nostro caro e amato tenore!" Corists, all people of the stage and supers, were all cleened up like a great occasion.

Everybody wait for "Pagliacci" being before a small concert in which the artists who tooked part were very bad.

We beginning and and as always the public dont under stand my frases but they enjoyed. I was not satisfied because I felted that there were not a communication between me and the public. First, because this one expect more of "Pagliacci" being paid three times the cost of ordinary ticket. Second, the concert were very bad and third there was a donkey with a little tiny bit of a car which make me nervous.

However, we arrived at the end of the first act. I dont know how I sang my arioso but the thing that I know is this: I find myself covered litterraly of flowers which came from stage, box, parterre and gallery and there was a terrible noise. After the fifth call I beginning to realize what was around me. The noise was the public who standing up, yelled as a man alone, and the women too who looked like crazy. I think there was many, many calls which makes me nearly feelin bad because the demostration were so strong that my heart was touched. Do you know what I was thinking and look for in the middle of such demostration? You! Yes, my eyes goes around the sala traying to find the box with my Doro. You were not there! I think if you were there you certainly cry of joy.

Funny, the same things you write to Mimmi was in my last letter to him. It seams he dont care for studio. Worse for him. I have done for him my best and it will not be my fault if he becomes an ass.

How many, many soprises you have for me? I hope lots. I kiss the little handkerchief of you.

I love you.

>Good night
>Rico

He sang Aïda in the bull ring on October 26.

Mexico City.
Oct. 26, 1919. 830 p.m.

My only sweetest Doro;

Here I am after the performance of Aida which was really triumph. There were some univeness but we finished the performance very well. I will describe you how everything goes.

Today was a beautiful day with the sunshine terribly hot. We beginning the performance and at moment to go on the stage this was illuminated plenety by the sun. I had like a shower of rays in my eyes terribly hot. Like Swedish bath. Then I was forced to close my eyes and impossible to look the condocter. The basso, worse than a bad corist, beginning to sing, with a voice like an old dog, doing "WHAU WHAU!!" Both things made me nervous and I beginning to sing "Celeste Aida" with my eyes closed and a bag of sunshine on my face. Impossible to sing well and my aria was sang without feeling and for a chance I dont make a terrible crak before the end. I finisched well and had a good applause. But the public understand that I was not satysfide and I think himself was the same because the ovation was not enthuiastic. The second scene was same thing and there was not enthusiasm even that I sang very well. Sombody told me that the cause was the basso.

The scene of the triumph passed. Then came the scene of the Nilo [Nile]. I mounted myself and taked my public. There were many calls and people were crazy. I dont know the exact words to express what the public doit. Heats, umbrellas, hendekacifs, canes all in the aria, and a shouts that arrived in heaven. I think

133

many people will have no voice for many days.

I must give my soul to take the public.

I will leave you for tomorrow.

You will excuse me, yes? Thanks.

All my love with all my soul.

Yours
Rico.

Mexico City Bucareli 85
Oct 27th 1919 10:30 a.m.

My adorable Doro:

Now I have no pain because I am here with you, my Doro, who I call every moment going around for the house. Yes, every moment, and when I dont expect, my lips pronounce and call you in this way, "Doro, mia, where are you?"

I never send you a message without kisses; you sometimes forgat so. . . . Good for K. to have sold the property. The things now is to know how to keep the money.

Again your father makes you angry? God likes to do that and we must obey His volonty! Ah! The old man is terrible! I dont know why he must have such a bad temper. I think that he never thinks that he must die. I think he never were kind with anybody. And think that I have a good feeling for him!

My great and immense love.

Your own
Rico

Mia adorata Doro:

At half past twelve I went to the Italian consul for the visa to the passport. There were a little trouble. Here all the offices closed at one o'clock and being arrived to the consulate little late, I told to Zirato to go up and see if we was in time and I wait in the auto. Little late, and come and said to me, "The consul want see you." I went out, and in going upstairs I find the consul, or vice-consul what he was, and with a bad temper and manners told me, "It is after one and the office is closed." Quigly I understand that something wrong happened and with the nice manners, I said to this little bist (because he was little and ogly) "You are right, and I will come back this afternoon. Three sharp." Zirato was nervous. It is from many days that he is nervous and I dont know why. Himself said that sometime he have not any volonty to work, and give the attribution to the change of the weather.

At three I went to the consulate. I find the vice-consul very kind and different from this morning. Both we want an explication and, being very polite, he told me that if he dont regestered the passaport this morning was because the man who goes up (Zirato) went in with bad manners and talking very loud. I excuse Zirato in telling that he is a little deft and then everythings was alright.

But, between us, is a little time that Zirato dont act any more as he must do. Near, he is all attentive, and far, he act like he is Caruso. I think Mexico goes in his head and tourned upside down. Nevermind. This is not my business, but if he continue like that he must go away. I feel sorry. Prehaps he change.

I hope God will be good with us and give me long life to be with you. Today week I will be near the American frontier and you can imagine with what anxiety I am looking for the day I will be close to you.

Do you know that every night, during the night and in the morning and during the day, I call you with high voice? Yes, dear, like a crazy I say, "Doro! Where are you?" Nobody answer! I feel so sad after, and mentally I say, "She is home but I hear her steps around me!"

Today in a week I will be only three days far from you.

Good night, goodnight I leave you for good now. Be quite on your chaise-long, and let me be near you on my knees to tell you I love you.

Rico

He sang a concert for the benefit of the Educational Fund of Mexico City on the 28th, and on the 30th *Manon Lescaut*. His farewell performance consisted of the third act of *L'Elisir d'amore*, the third act of *Martha* and the first act of *Pagliacci*. After the performance he telegraphed me: "Ovation after each aria and great, very great demonstration at the end, reaching delirium. Twenty-five thousand people. Am happy have been here and knowing this country and enthusiastic people that gave me continually great sensations."

* * *

And then he came home. It was wonderful.

Since we had written to each other all the details of each day, we didn't have to waste time repeating them—we could start living from the first moment we were together again. Everything Enrico said had to do with the present or the future, not with the past. I have never known anyone who had this unique virtue. With him I never had that impatient feeling, "You wrote me all that, don't tell me again."

He brought me all sorts of presents—linen, jewels, fans and lace. I loved them all and soon felt that he had never been away. Fucito was playing *La Juive* again in the studio. I knew the music now and sang it on my side of the house. Sometimes when Enrico suddenly appeared in the doorway and said in his unforgettable voice, "Ah, there you are, my Doro!" I felt the whole world lift to a heaven of happiness and I could find no words to tell him how much he meant to me. I could only say, "Oh, how I wish you were poor and didn't sing better than anyone else. Then you would know how much I love you."

Chapter Six

ENRICO hadn't had a day's rest since his return from Mexico, but for the moment his headaches had stopped and he was well and full of energy. At night before going to sleep he would read over once his lines in *La Juive*—he never actually studied them. He said he learned them in the night if his eyes saw them just before he slept. Every morning he rehearsed this opera at the Metropolitan, for he was to sing it ten days after he opened the season in *Tosca*. Besides these rehearsals he had to make records in Camden for the Victor Company. This was his hardest work, far more difficult than singing an opera. He hated every minute of it. "My voice is cold and heavy in the morning," he said, "and I don't feel to sing."

The first records Enrico ever made were not for the Victor Company. He had already experimented in Italy in 1896 on wax cylinders and a recording machine that was sent down from Germany. During the recording the primitive machine broke down and another had to be sent for from Berlin. In 1898 he made other recordings for a small Italian company which was later taken over by Victor.

His first recordings for the Victor Company were made in 1903 in Carnegie Hall, where the recording laboratory was then situated, and since he had no contract he was paid in cash. The friendship between him and Mr. Calvin Goddard Child, head of the Victor recording department, began at this epoch. His first ten recordings—all operatic arias—were: "Vesti la giubba"

(Pagliacci), "Celeste Aïda" (Aïda), "Una furtiva lagrima" (L'Elisir d'amore), "La donna è mobile" (Rigoletto), "E lucevan le stelle" (Tosca), "Recondita armonia" (Tosca), "Le Rêve" (Massenet's Manon), "Di quella pira" (Il Trovatore), and the "Siciliano" (Cavalleria rusticana). The popularity of these recordings secured for Enrico his first Victor contract.

CARUSO MAKING A RECORD (courtesy Gramophone Co., Ltd.)

At the Victor studio in Camden, New Jersey, he sang into a short square horn connected with the recording machine. The operator, who was working the machine behind a partition, made signs to him through a little window. No one was ever allowed to go behind that partition because it contained the secrets of the Victor Company. The musicians who accompanied Enrico sat on stools of graded heights at the back of the room. Their relative positions controlled the volume of sound, as there were no amplifiers in those days.

He began by singing with the orchestra. Then he told them

any changes he wanted and sang the song again. "Good. Now we start," he said, and made a sign to the operator. When he had finished, the record was immediately played back to him and he discussed it with Mr. Child. Had it recorded well? Would the public like it? This record couldn't be replayed because it was made of wax and destroyed itself in the playing. Over and over he sang the same song. Sometimes a violin was too loud; then the violinist climbed down from his stool and retired to another farther back. If Enrico disliked the way a certain tone of his voice had registered, he insisted on making still another recording. At last, after two hours, a satisfactory record might be achieved. This was used to make the copper master record from which the black rubber ones would be stamped. Each time he went to Camden he sang at most only two or three songs, and although he longed to get back home he never rushed through the work or let anything pass that might be improved. Two days later when Mr. Child brought samples of the finished recordings to New York, he and Enrico listened to them once more. This was the most important test of all, for both men had to agree on the perfection of every note before the record could be offered to the public. If they didn't agree, it was destroyed and Enrico had to return to Camden and do it all over again.

Once he had to sing "Cujus animam" from Rossini's Stabat Mater many times before he was satisfied with the recording. When at last it was finished, he drew a pearl stickpin from his tie and handed it to the exhausted trumpet player. "You merit reward," he said. "In the end I thought you also would crack."

Although Enrico denied having a favorite opera, I know he had favorites among his recordings. Of his Neapolitan songs he liked best "A vuchella," by Tosti, and he often sang it at his concerts as an encore. He considered "Rachel" from La Juive the best of his operatic arias, and "*Solenne in quest' ora*" from *La Forza del Destino*, with Scotti, the best of his duets. At home he often played "Love Me or Not." He had sung it in English and called it "our love song." To teach him the English pronunciation I read the syllables to him, pronouncing them slowly and distinctly. When his ear had recorded each vowel and consonant, he wrote down the sounds phonetically in his clear, careful writing.

He liked everything about "Over There"—words, music, spirit and George M. Cohan. Once Mr. Cohan dined with us, ate only crackers and milk and told us excruciatingly funny stories of his life in a soft melancholy voice. Often Enrico listened to jazz records. "It is funny and interesting," he would say. He liked both Victor Herbert and his songs. "He has melody," he said, "and that is important for such kind of music." The grave magnificence of Handel's "Largo" moved him deeply. Simple songs like the "*Campane a sera*" carried him back to Italy and his home; he seemed again to be hearing the vesper bell of the old monastery on a still summer evening.

As a wedding present the Victor Company sent us a black and gold Chinese lacquer phonograph. On the inside of the red lid was attached a gold record of "*La donna è mobile*," because this was the first song he had recorded for them, in 1903.

Up to January, 1920, royalties amounting to $1,825,000 had been paid to Enrico by the Victor Company.

* * *

It was now the middle of December and time for the baby to be born. We had been considering hundreds of names for her, but it was only the night before her birth that Enrico suddenly decided she must be called Gloria—"because," he said, "she will be my crowning glory."

She was born on the night of December 18, 1919, at half-past ten. The first words I heard afterward were, "Dearest, it's a little girl." As he held her in his arms he announced that, besides the name of Gloria, she must have others—Grazianna, in gratitude to his mother whose name was Anna; Ameriga, because she was born in America; Vittoria, because we won the war, and Maria for the Virgin Mary. Enrico ordered champagne for the entire staff of the hotel and gave tiny Gloria a drop from the end of his little finger. His happiness was triumphant. The following night he sang *L'Elisir d'amore* and the gallery shouted, "*Viva papa!*"

One morning a month later we were in the nursery watching Nanny bathe and dress the baby. "What you put those things on her for?" he asked. "How you keep her little back strong with those things? You don't swaddle?" "No, Rico dear, she wears dresses." "Very funny indeed. In Italy we swaddle. You not like to swaddle, Puschina?" He picked her up and carried her to the window, pried her mouth open and gazed down her throat. "Look, Doro, she is exactly like me. Maybe she sing—maybe not, but her throat is the same as mine."

I watched their faces in the sunlight. They looked so extraordinarily alike that I wanted to cry.

* * *

The Metropolitan Opera Company gave performances in Philadelphia every other Tuesday. They traveled in a special train, and on Caruso nights we went with them. Enrico was always silent on the journey, because he was going to sing, but after the performance, on the way back to New York, he was in high spirits and communicated his exhilaration to us all. We took along big baskets of chicken and veal cutlets, salad, quantities of fruit and wine and cheese, and sweet loaves of fresh French bread. Enrico

142

would invite his special friends—Scotti, Amato, De Luca, Rothier, Didur—and other members of the company to have supper with us and tell them stories of his youth. He recalled the old days when he had to sing two operas on Sundays at the Teatro Mercadante in Naples, and the summer season in Salerno when he was so hungry that during the entr'actes he let down a little basket on a string from his dressing-room window for the sandwich vendor to fill. He told us of the night in Brussels when there wasn't even standing room left and music-loving students of the university, unable to get into the theater, gathered in the street and shouted up to his dressing room; he opened the window and sang his aria to them before going down to the stage. There was also his story of the first time he ever sang in a theater in a little town near Naples when he was just nineteen. He was hissed off the stage because, not having expected to sing that night, he had drunk too much good red wine with his supper. He returned to his little room, certain that his career was ended, and his despair was so great that he even thought of killing himself. But the following night the audience so disliked the substitute tenor that they called for "the little drunkard." Enrico was sent for in haste and made his first success that night. The next morning when photographers arrived to take pictures of the promising young singer, they found him naked in bed—he had sent his only shirt to be washed. He draped the bedspread around his shoulders and posed for his photograph with a proud and stern expression. This picture was the first ever published of Caruso.

* * *

Enrico loved to tell stories, but he never gossiped, nor did he listen to gossip. "Why do they talk and waste their time?" he said one night after a dinner party. "If there is something good to say, speak—otherwise be quiet." As he hated being lionized, social functions in his honor had no place in his busy life. A well-known Philadelphia hostess once telephoned to ask if she might give a dinner and ball for the young bride. My first reaction was, "Oh, what fun!" I had never been to a ball, nor had anyone ever given a dinner just for me. But before I could speak Enrico said to Zirato, "What she want to bother us for? Does she not know I work? Tell her that we not like people, and be sure she understand. She does not do this for us, but for her." I felt a little disappointed but said nothing. Enrico looked at me. "You feel sad, my Doro? I am perhaps selfish? It is that I enjoy so to be alone with you." No party, no matter how gorgeous, could give me such happiness as being alone with Enrico. And he had just said that he wanted to be alone with me. I could never get used to it.

Enrico was a musician who had no time for music. We never went together to hear opera. I don't believe he had heard one for twenty years, except those in which he himself sang; and even then he never stood in the wings to listen to the other singers. We never went to symphony concerts either. Once we went to a recital—the debut of Tito Schipa, who was giving a program of Neapolitan songs. We arrived late, sat in the back of the hall where no one could see us and left in fifteen minutes. "Why did we go at all?" I asked. "Because he is a tenor. But it's all right," he said cryptically.

Enrico didn't play the piano, he could strike only a few chords; but he never said he regretted not being able to play. As he concentrated on only one thing at a time, he wouldn't have accompanied himself in any case, for he refused to divide his attention.

No amateur accompanist ever played for him, nor did he ever sing "for fun" at parties. His contract with the Metropolitan forbade his singing anywhere unless he had official permission. I know of only one time that he broke this rule. We had gone to a benefit vaudeville performance, given for soldiers and sailors, at the Manhattan Opera House. We thought no one could see us, seated in the back of a stage box, but a boy in the front row called out, "There's Caruso!" The performance stopped, the audience shouted and stamped and the manager came to our box. "Mr. Caruso, they want you to sing 'Over There.' " Enrico didn't hesitate but left me immediately and went on to the stage. When he had finished, the audience wouldn't let him go. Finally, waving and calling "No more," he hurried back to me. "We must leave quickly," he whispered. "I must go and tell Gatti I broke my contract." I waited in the car outside the stage door while he talked with Gatti. When he came out he was beaming. "He excuse me," he said.

The only person to whom Enrico ever gave a singing lesson was Ricardo Martin. He didn't like to teach, nor did he think he did it well. He always said, "To sing is one thing, to teach is another. How can I explain how I do? I hold my chest up—so. And my stomach in—so. And my sit-down in—so. And then I sing." He listened without comment while others explained the "Caruso method" to him—"because I must be polite." Once after an interview with an earnest professor of voice, he said, "He knows more than me. When he teaches he takes an umbrella and when he opens it the pupils sing 'EEE-EEE-AAAAA,' and when he closes it slowly, slowly, they go 'AAA-AAA-EEE!' "

Enrico told me that when he sang he never thought of his throat or the position of his tongue. He considered words to be of first importance in singing. "I think to the words of my aria, not to the music, because first is written the libretto and is the reason of the composer to put the melody, like foundation for a house. When people think I sing freely and think I take the life easy on the stage, they mistake. At such time I am working at the top of my strength. I must not show that I work when I sing—that is what is art."

The cavities within Enrico's face were extraordinary. The depth, width and height of the roof of his mouth, the broad cheekbones and flat even teeth, the wide forehead above wide-set

CARUSO SELF-PORTRAIT

eyes—this spacious architecture gave him his deep resonance of tone. He could put an egg in his mouth, close his lips, and no one would guess that an egg was there. His chest was enormous and he could expand it nine inches "Does he never breathe?" people sometimes asked as a phrase, unbroken by a breath, went on and on to its final supreme note. But his vocal cords in themselves were no more remarkable than those of most singers.

When he was asked what were the requisites of a great singer he said, "A big chest, a big mouth, ninety per cent memory, ten per cent intelligence, lots of hard work and something in the heart."

His memory was phenomenal. He knew sixty-seven roles, and

146

to his repertoire of more than five hundred songs he was continually adding others.

As he grew older his voice became richer, heavier, darker, and this development gave him full mastery of great dramatic roles like Samson, Eleazar and John of Leyden, while he still excelled in lyric operas like *Martha* and *L'Elisir d'amore*. He sang in French, Italian, Spanish and English but never consented to sing in German even when so requested by the Kaiser. On that occasion he told the Berlin press: "Italian is the most simple language to sing. It has five vowels pure, and very few consonants. It is impossible for me to sing in German because the consonants repeat too often, and because the sharp accents stop me to phrase properly and take from my voice the brilliancy. Foreign artists who sing German have better technique than me—that is all."

Once in an interview he answered the question "At what age is a singer's voice at its best?": "For women I cannot say, but for tenors I think between the ages of thirty and forty-five. Before thirty they have not either the art or the heart. After that they ought to have both, and if they have the voice, good. When I was a boy of ten in Italy I sang, and sang well. When I was a man of twenty I sang, and perhaps sang better. When I was a man of thirty I had the voice, the experience, the art, and I sang better still."

* * *

Although by the time he was twenty-one Enrico had sung publicly at some small theaters in the vicinity of Naples, he didn't consider that he had made his official debut until November 16, 1894, when he sang in the opera *L'Amico Francesco* at the Nuova in Naples. He received eighty lire a night and was engaged for four performances. The opera wasn't a success, but the young tenor was considered rather good.

Twenty-five years later, on March 22, 1919, his jubilee was

147

celebrated at the Metropolitan—his five hundred and fiftieth performance on that stage. Poor Enrico dreaded that night, for he had to sing an act from three different operas—*L'Elisir*, *Pagliacci* and *Le Prophète*. As he left for the theater he said, "Everyone will enjoy but me."

At the end of the performance I went backstage to watch from the wings. The curtain rose. Enrico had changed to evening clothes and was sitting on a little gold chair close to the footlights, formally encircled by all the singers and the entire personnel of the Metropolitan. He looked alarmed. He listened to all the flowery tributes, not a word of which, other than about his voice, did he believe. At the back of the stage a large table was piled high with presents—a silver vase from the directors of the Metropolitan, another from the musicians of the orchestra, a loving cup from the chorus, a huge illuminated parchment from the box owners of the opera houses of New York, Philadelphia and Brooklyn, a silver epergne from the Victor Company, a gold medal from Gatti and many other tributes. As a climax he was presented with the flag of the city of New York, symbol of five and a half million people. He accepted it as simply as a drink of water and made a tortured little speech. I wondered what he was feeling . . . if he was remembering the boy who, for a few lire, had copied music at night in the streets of Naples.

The jubilee overflowed into our apartment. When we got home Enrico made helpless little gestures with his hands toward the gifts that covered all the tables and chairs of the salon. "What we do with all these things, Doro?" He was grateful for each individual offering, but the total result was staggering. A monstrous hand-made rug of coarse black wool woven with gigantic red flowers covered half the floor. Silver cups and punchbowls, picture frames and desk sets, stood between

148

masses of American Beauty roses. There were a dozen canes and umbrellas with gold or silver or ivory knobs, onyx cuff links with large diamonds, eleven eighteenth-century enameled antique jeweled watches, oil paintings of flowers, fruits and dead birds, and portraits of both of us embroidered on silk, framed in bright gilt. There were boxes of poker chips and chessmen—games he never played—and Corona Corona cigars, which he never smoked. There were innumerable gold pencils, gold pens, gold cigarette cases, gold paper knives, and many framed tributes written on illuminated parchment, signed with hundreds of musicians' names. On the center of the table, on a mammoth silver tray, hundreds of telegrams were piled between great horse-shoes of roses tied with ribbons of red, white, blue and green, the combined colors of America and Italy.

"*Dio mio*, where we put all this?" Enrico said. "Ah, well, the public liked, and for the Metropolitan it was good advertising. And now I wish to sleep."

Chapter Seven

ENRICO was made in two parts—man and genius. My understanding of him depended on my recognition of which part, at a given moment, was motivating his actions. I couldn't always distinguish instantly between the man and the genius, and the result on one occasion was both startling and pitiful.

His jealousy astonished me, although he had told me when we married, "You will not talk to any man when I am not with you." "Not even to my brother's friends?" "No, not even; for if you are seen, who will know he is the friend of your brother?" This request didn't even seem unreasonable to me; it was only another opportunity to do something for him.

The spring before we sailed for Italy we went to Atlanta with the Metropolitan Opera Company. On the evening after Enrico's first performance two old friends of his, whom I hadn't met, invited us to a dinner and dance. The night was warm, sweet and starry and tables were set around the dance floor under trees hung with lanterns. We sat at the most conspicuous table with our host Jim, a big fat jolly man, and his wife Fanny May, gay, plump and pretty. I could see that they both adored Enrico.

After dinner when the orchestra began to play I felt a sudden agony of shyness sweep over me. "What am I doing here," I thought desperately, "among all these people I have never seen before, who are staring and smiling at me simply because I am married to the greatest tenor in the world?" At that moment Enrico asked me to dance. I looked up at him and refused—he had become a stranger too. "All right, a little later. Fanny May?" They danced away together. I watched them whirl around alone on the floor, but when other couples joined them my shyness left me and I felt natural and happy again. My host asked me to dance and I accepted at once. Halfway around the floor Enrico saw us and as we passed he said, "I wish to speak with you when you finish." He was waiting for me at the table. "We go home now," he said. "But, Enrico, we can't do that to Fanny May." "Never mind, I fix. Get now your coat." I was completely mystified.

Back in our sitting room at the hotel he burst forth, "What for you dance with that man after you refuse me? Why you do such a thing—that fat man?" "But, Rico, he is your friend and our host." "He is not my friend that you do such a thing. I have no friends. And I—am I nothing? Am I not important—only the host important?" He was shouting. I tried to explain, but his fury mounted with each word I spoke. "So, that is it. You not like to be married to Caruso!" I burst into tears.

Then came the transformation. The blaze of anger left his eyes and they filled with tears. "Ai me," he groaned, "what I say to you? What have I done? Oh, bad, bad am I to make you cry!" Rushing across the room, he beat his head against the wall. Blood and tears ran down his face. I implored him to stop, but it was useless. He kept sobbing, "So sorry, Doro—you excuse?" I washed his poor head, helped him to bed and sat by him, patting him and saying, "There, there, Rico," until he fell asleep. I understood instinctively that it was not Caruso the man indulging in a jealous scene, but Caruso the genius whose nature moved in the same lavish dimensions as his art.

We never referred to that dreadful night again. Months later he said, "I wish you to become very fatty so no one look at you." Then he sighed.

* * *

Each time Enrico came in from the street he changed all his clothes, and unless he was receiving people he never wore a conventional suit in the house. He wore dark red, green or blue brocaded coats with sashes, slate-gray silk trousers and soft shirts. When we were first married I was surprised at the number and variety of clothes in his wardrobe. One closet held eighty pairs of shoes, another fifty suits. "Why do you have so many?" I asked. "Two reasons," he said. "First reason, I like. Second reason, other people like. Also I give to people who ask."

A few days after we were married my father sent me a small steamer trunk containing everything I had left at home. There was not much in it—a few books and pictures, my two dresses and my winter coat. Enrico came in as I was unpacking. "Ah, your little things you do." He touched the coat. "You have a warmer, a fur?" "Oh, yes, in storage. It's nice and warm." "I see." His voice was very gentle. "I like you not keep these things, my Doro. I like give you everything. Today I like you have another fur coat." That afternoon he took me to Joseph's on Fifth Avenue. It was the first time I had ever been in such a shop— gray, soft and perfumed. We sat with the manager in front of a little stage. He awed me, but Enrico was at ease as usual. One by one mannequins came out on the stage in sable, ermine and chinchilla, in moleskin, broadtail and beaver. There were muffs and hats to match. "Which you like, Doro?" Heavens, they all looked so expensive! I had never dreamed of such furs. The moleskin was the shortest and probably cost less than the others. I said, "Perhaps the little moleskin?" "Yes, it is pretty," said Enrico. He turned to the manager. "We will take them all."

As I knew nothing about smart clothes, Enrico selected my entire wardrobe and even supervised the fittings. Since his ideas were on a grand scale, he began by ordering sixty-nine costumes— fifteen evening gowns, twelve afternoon dresses, eight tailored suits, six topcoats, twelve evening wraps, four tea gowns, twelve house pajamas. As I went to the opera twice a week and had to wear a different dress each time, my evening gowns had to be replaced several times during the season. All morning and all afternoon, every day for weeks, I went to fittings. After the first hour I was dizzy from revolving and unable to stand still any longer. But the pitiless fitters continued to pin, baste, drape and cut until I wondered how I could bear my grim future of beautiful clothes.

Once I admired a costume hat Enrico wore in *Rigoletto*—it had a limp red velvet crown, a wide brim faced with blue satin and a long white ostrich feather drooping over the ear. Unfortunately my admiration made a deep impression. About a month later, when I was recovering from pneumonia and still in bed, he knocked on my door, calling, "I have a present for you." He came in, followed by Mario and Enrichetta, all carrying large boxes. In the boxes were six replicas of his *Rigoletto* hat which he had ordered Tappé to copy in six different colors. His idea was that I wear them in the street—which I did, of course. They weren't very becoming and I had great difficulty finding clothes that could be worn with them.

Enrico ordered my jewels in the same prodigal way, describing exactly what he wanted and choosing meticulously from among the designs submitted to him. In a month a large jewel case was filled with sets of every kind of gem. They matched my costumes and became simple accessories, like handkerchiefs and gloves. A safe was built into the wall of our bedroom, and only Enrico and I had the combination. There we kept the jewels and also his bags of American gold pieces "for emergencies."

On opera nights, after choosing the jewels I was to wear, I would put the case back into the safe and drive to the theater, three blocks away. By the middle of the first act my thoughts would fix on the safe—had I closed it? As soon as Zirato came to escort me backstage I would implore him to go to the apartment and look at the safe. If he found I had left it open I would rush home to close it, hoping that Enrico wouldn't notice my absence. I felt it unfair to give Zirato this responsibility in case anything should be missing.

* * *

Enrico was ruthless when singers came to him for criticism, and scarcely a day passed without his listening to an audition. Some of the voices were good, others frightful. Society women were the most trying—I remember one who insisted on singing her entire repertoire, even after Enrico had told her that her voice wasn't suited for opera. "But what is wrong with my voice?" she insisted. "It is too old," he said bluntly.

One day the Marchesa C., a ravishingly beautiful woman, and her little husband came to see us. Enrico had known them both in Italy. She had sung professionally throughout Europe, accompanied at the piano by her husband. She was to give a Debussy recital at the Princess Theatre for a smart audience, and hoped to be engaged for private soirees later on. If Enrico would only go to her concert, she was sure it would be a success.

We went and sat in the front row. It was a matinee, and the audience, chiefly women, was thrilled at seeing Caruso. Many pretended to know him, fluttering their eyes and tittering. "Who are they, so foolish?" he muttered as we sat down.

On the stage were potted palms, a piano and a tall Italian chair. There was polite applause as the Marchesa entered. Dressed in black velvet, long and tight, she glided to the chair and sank down. She had hair like black silk, smoothed down on either side of a lotus-white face, a nose and mouth by Praxiteles, and long eyes enormous in their blue shadows. She held a muff on her lap

154

and sat as still as glass. Her little husband whispered in and effaced himself at the piano. Then she began to sing Debussy.

The audience sat hypnotized—all but Enrico. He rolled his eyes and pushed up his nose with the knob of his cane. After it was all over the husband met us in the lobby, trembling with excitement.

"Come with me," he said, "there are crowds waiting, but she will see you."

"I go home," said Enrico.

"But——" said the little man.

"I go home," said Enrico again and added over his shoulder, "You can come to dinner tonight."

At dinner Enrico laughed, talked and told stories without stopping. He never mentioned the concert. The Marchesa became more and more unresponsive. She waited until the coffee was served to say, "Well, Caruso, what did you think of my recital?"

"Beautiful," said Enrico without hesitation. "You had a great success."

"Yes, but what did you think about me?"

"You were very effective—the chair—the muff—everything. I tell you they liked very much."

"But what about my voice, my singing?"

Enrico's expression changed. "You want to know my opinion of your voice as Caruso the artist or Caruso the friend?"

Her voice was high as she answered, "Artist, of course."

"Well, then, I tell you. You do not sing because you do not know how."

She was furious. "How can you say that? I have studied seven years with Jean de Reszke!"

"Then, madame, you both wasted seven years. You have no voice, you know nothing about singing. But you will be engaged because you look nice."

Immediately she rose from the table and left the house.

The next day Mrs. Belmont and Mrs. Reginald de Koven called on us. They had been to the recital and wanted to know what Enrico thought of it. If he said it was good, they would ask the Marchesa to sing in their houses.

"She is most effective and made a great success," said Enrico. "You not make a mistake." They had thought so too, they said, and went away pleased.

"You see, Doro, she get the work. But she had not the sense to keep quiet after I show I not want to talk. She made me hurt her, otherwise she repeat to someone that I say she sing well and they maybe know singing and say, 'Caruso is a stupid—he cannot tell good voice from bad.' This I cannot let happen for my name as an artist. Always I must tell the truth—if they insist."

* * *

During his long career many legends grew up around the name of Caruso. Some of them were fantastic, some were true, others held a kernel of truth; but, true or false, they have continued and increased year after year. I have often been questioned about these legends, and this list of facts will answer some of the questions:

Enrico was five feet nine inches tall (a half inch taller than I) and weighed 175 pounds.

His complexion was cream, without color in the cheeks.

His hair was black, coarse and straight.

His body was hard but not muscular.

His hands were large and strong, with square fingers.

His feet were small and broad.

He could not run well because of the formation of the Achilles tendon.

He took two baths a day.

156

He bathed his face with witch hazel.

He did not use face powder except on the stage.

He used Caron perfumes; he walked around the apartment with a large atomizer, spraying the rooms with scent.

He weighed three pounds less after each performance.

He did not lie down to rest during the day.

He did not ride, play golf or tennis, go for long walks, or do setting-up exercises in the morning.

He never learned to drive a car

He did not overeat.

He never ate five plates of spaghetti for lunch! His lunch was vegetable soup with the meat of chicken left in, and a green salad.

For dinner he usually had a minute steak, two green vegetables and ice cream.

When he was to sing, he ate only the white meat of chicken or two small lamb chops.

He ate the crust of bread with every meal.

He loved ice cream and custard.

His favorite vegetable was raw fennel, which he ate like fruit.

He did not eat candies or chocolate.

He did not drink beer, highballs, milk or tea; he drank two or three quarts of bottled mineral water a day. Sometimes he took a little wine, and the only cocktail he liked was an Alexander.

He did not chew gum.

He smoked two packages of Egyptian cigarettes a day, always in a holder.

He loved children and dogs.

He would have no pets in the city.

He would have no caged birds at the villa in Signa.

He would not permit songbirds to be shot on his property.

He never shattered either a mirror or a wineglass with his voice, as has been stated.

When he was well he went to bed at midnight and slept eight hours.

He took no medicines of any kind except, the night before he sang, half a bottle of Henri's powdered magnesia in water.

He did not make his debut as a baritone.

He never employed a claque, although he was warmly attached to old Schol, chief-of-claque at the Metropolitan.

In all his life he sang in only one amateur performance—*Cavalleria rusticana*, given in Naples in 1892, admission free.

He always retained his Italian citizenship.

Above all countries he preferred to sing in America.

* * *

The mysterious headaches from which Enrico had suffered three months before in Mexico came on again in January—not daily, but often enough to keep his nerves at high tension. At this time, to be obliged to sing in the morning was nothing less than an affliction. He had to rise early, sing exercises, treat his throat, put on formal morning clothes, which he hated. One morning when he was to sing at a Bagby musicale at the Waldorf he woke with a blinding attack. As he dressed I watched the vein swell in his temple and the pulse begin to beat so strongly in his neck that his head vibrated visibly. He tried on at least ten collars before finding one he could endure. At last he said, "Let me lie down." His eyes were inflamed and nearly closed. Zirato held ice against his wrists, but it didn't help the pain. "Shall we telephone to Bagby?" I asked Zirato in a whisper. He shook his head, "Not yet." Slowly Enrico sat up. "Come, we go. I must sing."

When he came out on the stage he showed no signs of suffering. He finished his program and then sang encore after encore. Finally he said, "Thank you, but I must stop because I have such a hunger—I sing without breakfast, you know." This intimacy charmed his audience—the great singer Caruso, divided from them by the footlights, had become a warm personal friend. As I was leaving I heard one woman say, "Dear thing, isn't he?" Her companion answered, "So charming—I know him well." His voice had delighted them, but his words had made him their own. They hadn't remarked the beating vein in his temple. Enrico was a good showman.

* * *

At the end of April he was to leave for Cuba to sing two months of opera in Havana with Bracale's company. I couldn't go with him because Gloria was too young to travel and we would never have dreamed of leaving her behind.

The day before he left we lunched at the Casino in Central Park. I watched a big open Packard drive up to the door, a beautiful gray car with green wheels and green leather seats. Later I said to Enrico, "Did you notice that beautiful car? I think it had a special body." He said he hadn't noticed it. When we had finished lunch I waited outside while Enrico paid the check. The park was lovely in the spring and we drove around it twice before returning home. "Look," I said as I stepped out in front of our hotel, "there's the Packard I saw at the Casino." It was parked near the entrance, and Enrico stood beside me a moment admiring it. Then he said, "It is yours, my Doro. I bought it from its owner after lunch." I don't know why the owner was willing to sell it. Perhaps because Enrico offered him $12,000.

In the early evening I went into the studio and found him holding Gloria on his knees. Fucito was playing the piano and Enrico was beating time with the baby's little fist.

"I teach her a song—'Oh, Mr. Piper'—about a fairy queen," and he began to sing it softly. She rested against him, contented. "You see," he said, "she likes the father's voice." She was three months old.

Chapter Eight

AFTER Enrico had gone to Cuba I took Gloria, Nanny, my brother and his wife, their children and all the servants to Easthampton, Long Island, where we had rented a place for the summer. The house was long and low, with a large studio on the ground floor; upstairs, next to my bedroom, there was a workroom for Enrico which could be reached by a little staircase that led up from the gardens. These lovely gardens were famed for their great beds of pink zinnias and terraces of white iris that led down to a small lake and a rose-covered guesthouse. From the chauffeur's cottage at the entrance gate it was a ten-minute walk to the house, through woods and fields.

A week after our arrival I was startled to read in the papers that the Knickerbocker Hotel had been sold. When Enrico cabled me instructions I went to New York at once and transferred all our furniture to his gallery. He was extremely upset:

> Atlanta, Georgia
> April 27th
>
> My dearest Doro:
>
> Last night going in the restaurant for a little supper, the manager of this hotel stop me and told me the following, "Been the Knickerbocker sold, I beg you, if you like, to consider the proposition that the Biltmore Hotel made to you many years ago." I quite dont understand at beguinning but he showed me a newspaper in which was told that the Knickerbocker was sold

and will be change in office building. Let you immagine how I rest after such news. No supper and I goes down in a big prostration in thinking to you and all the trouble you will have.

Some day, go to, or write to Bowman of the Biltmore and tell that remembering Mr Caruso the offre which he does him many years ago, you personally like to be at the Biltmore and would like to fix everything before Mr Caruso will be back.

The proposition that was made to me was to give me a suite on the 18th floor for nothing. I refused because I dont like to live without pay in any place. Now if we will have a nice apartment there for less money of the Knickerbocker I think is not bad, being this hotel good situated for the emergency of the baby.

Now a little consideration. Since when Regan of the Knickerbocker had the idea to sell the hotel? If such things were in his mind before I left for Atlanta I think he was not kind with me because I had the time to pack everything myself and not put you in any trouble. I dont care for anything, only for you, my sweet Doro.

I send to my own blood, you and baby, heartling thoughts and thousands of kisses.

Your

Rico.

A few days later he wrote:

After all the exchange of telegrams between me, you, and Regan, it seams that Regan was offended for our sudenly decision and I was informed that he was unpleasant with you. I sent him a cable very gentle, in saying him, that all truble was caused by him because he dont inform me of the sale of the Knickerbocker at right time, and only after I give my disposition, he came out with this kindness. For consequence, his unpleasentness to you was out place. The only thing I am surprised that you dont answer him as he merit. But I understand that a lady must dont forget herself and for consequence leave the people where they born. The fault is mine because I must dont leave you alone! This is a lesson for me!

During the week he was in Atlanta he sang three performances —Samson, La Juive and L'Elisir d'amore. From Jacksonville he wrote:

I arrived here at 7 p.m. and was reconized by lots of people, with their smile on the lips. They make many round around me to see my face because as soon as somebody reconize me, I tourn my face to the other side and for consequence people tourn round many time.

Then I had your telegram and in reeding it my eyes became all wet, and when I answered it the man of the telegraph looked at me and ask if I had a cold. I said, "No, I am emotionated for the good news of my sweet little family." He said, "I understand very well, because I myself wrote the telegram which arrived from New York for you and myself was touched from the way which was written. It is so rare," he said, "to reed such things." I think he felt in love with you, or he was disappointed in his life because he talk and talk about happiness and sadness, for nearly half an hour. Until I was forced, with a blak face to ask him, "How much?" and then he understood and stopped.

We had to wait for the train about six hours and we pass the time to walk up and down, up and down, near the depot. Of course, as I have my name written on my face, I was reconized from everybody and the one who come and ask if I was he, I said, "No, I am his cosin" and everybody laugh and said, "You dont fool us because you are such a big personality that everybody knows you." I said, "Who, me? Thank you very much." Such things happen every moment in the train, and I am obliged to close myself in and sleep.

I miss you! I miss you! I am like a idorfobo * dog!

On the fifth of May he arrived in Havana and sent me his first impression: "Habana is a country that resembles to our Naples, old but with a caracter special because the constructions are made with 'porti cati' to be protected from the sun. The people are like the Spanish with a little of the smart of the United States."

During the next weeks his letters were filled with the difficulties he was having in Havana. The heat was exhausting, he scarcely slept at all, and for the first time in his life he had a toothache. He had once said to me, "Samson was strong because of his hair. My strong is in my teeth. When one goes away, I will go and Caruso will be finish." Across thousands of miles of space each of us felt the nervousness of the other.

* In these eight letters Enrico has added a new word to Italian and English. He meant "hydrophobic."

Hotel Sevilla Havana Cuba

May 5th, 1920 4/30 pm

My sweet Doro:

Two words in urry because I have rehearsal at 5 o'clock. I arrived here this morning at 7 o'clock, received by the best peoples of the city. When the boat arrived at the pier a long applause sound in the air. This come from hundreds peoples who was on the pier.

After I land there was the presentations and the compliments of the occasion.

In the car of the most prominent men, whom I know from long time in New York, I was brought to this hotel where I find many people who were in the Knickerbocker many years ago. They took care of my apartment for which I will pay 70 dollars a day without meals.

I had three hours meeting with newspaper men and lover music and ten o'clock I was able to have a bath and a little rest. At twelve o'clock, I was to the theatre to see about my dressing room.

8 p.m.

Dearest, just finished my rehearsal. It is very warm and I am so tired. Will close this few words because tomorrow morning early, the mail start for N.Y. I send to you and our Gloria my best love and affections and lots of kisses.

Your

Rico.

My Doro sweetheart:

It is the second day which I am here and seams that I am in the graces of the public. All the newspapers are full of news about me and during the few steps I made in walking everybody knows me and smile in saluting me. I meet many people whom knows me from New York and they are so proud that I came here and everybody try to be gentle with me and invitations of every kind.

We beguinning our rehearsal and the artists who took part in "Martha" with me, outside Barrientos, are astonished and they said that the public will be crazy. I hope so.

We will open the season next Wednesday because "Martha" is new for everybody of the cast.

Here is very warm and I prespire like I was in electric box. Nothing it is possible for me to were! If you see me now you will laugh. A bed sheet on me closed at my west by a strip of silk and let me look like an old Roman consul. My pores are always open and water come out like a river. I think I loose every day about ten pounds.

Too bad you dont bought the sheets. Remember the linens is never enough. Myself here I bought 12 sheets for my bed because I cannot sleep in cotton sheets. They are very ordinary but fresch. Then if you are in time to buy the sheets, as you said, buy, for I care very much for good linin for bed.

The people here are so slow in everything on account of the hot, for consequence you can immagine me with my quickness, how I stand.

Two days later his feeling of nervousness had increased:

I feel so afraid of all the things which I hear around here. I just finished to answer to a newspaper which wrote last night an article against me, in wishing me my Waterloo. Sometime I cannot let pas such things and for consequence I was obliged to answer in a very dignitiouse way, in sending bak the bad wishes. I do not understand why in the world must be people who try to wish bad look to the one who try to work onestly. Well, I wish that everything will be alright and let such people die of envy.

Here, down in the street is a store of records, and my dear, from the morning to the night they play every kind of discs and they put mine very high like a trumpet and the crowd stop the circulation.

This morning when I went out lots boys who came out from the school reconized me and do the same things what boys in the school in 44th Street used to do. There was a policeman who saved me because all this boys beguinning to be insolent in asking me to sing for they.

In the night it is impossible for me to sleep on account of the hot. I been to the Casino and as ever I loosed three hundred dollars without have the pleasure to gain a number.

Darling, you have Gloria with you, and that let pass your time quickly, but me—what a life! I cannot walk any more here. Men, women, boys, girls, everybody knows me and they acting like bad children. They calls me, they follow me, pass before my steps, and lots of annoyance. Sometimes I wish give lots of knock in the face of everybody. I am looking for the end of the season like the people who are near to die and wish to be saved. No more, sweetheart! I will stay always with my two Puschine darlingest!

It is possible that Gloria notice my absence, and for that she cry and make you cry too? Perhaps! We dont know what pass in her little breans!

You talk so sweetly of our dearest Gloria that my eyes cry.

Your

Rico.

Hotel Sevilla Habana Cuba.

May 8 1920, 9 a.m.

My Doro, my sweet love:

Your sweet letter of the third just arrived and make me so happy. How dearest you are! The happy one am I! I think this is the most sweet letter which you have write me in Italian. Your Italian, cara mia, is an art. Your expressions are so delightful that makes me feel something in my spine.

Your Italian is better of my English because you know all the words and your idee (How do you speel this word, Idey, aidy, or idy?) are perfectly put down and compresinbly, instead me, to write a period take me long time and I go crazy to find the right word. Sometime I say to myself, "Why are you so stupid?" and I have a fight with Caruso because he say, "I cannot do many things alltogether." I excuse him and then we try to do our best, in working very hard. But been you so kind with me, I am encouraged and I will go on better and better every day.

Sweet Gloria! She is like the mother, absolutely. Dont make me jealous with your way of talking about her! I wish to be there

167

with you and enjoy of what our sweet baby doo. I am looking forward to come home to enjoy, with you, of the caresses of this little angel.

Dearest love, I embrace you with all my soul.

Your
Rico

Hotel Sevilla Havana Cuba
Monday May 10th 1920 4 p.m.

My Doro darling love:

Your letter from the fourth arrived and I thank you for the joy which you give me in let me reed you for so long.

It is the very best moment in my stupid life which I have here. When your letter arrive I close all the doors and for many times I reed your letter from the beguinning to the end. It is the only confort which I have and I am very much obliged to you, my own love.

The work here beguinning and how hard it is! Yesterday at 1 p.m. until 6 I had stage rehersal and in working I dont make any attention to enything else but in the end I realized in what condition I was. Everything I had on was very wait and attacked on me. Tonight will be the same thing because we have the general rehersal. Immagine what will be at the performance. I am so afraid for that, and I wish to go to sleep tonight, and wake up tomorrow near you.

I meet many people here and everybody is very kind with me but I wish to be far away from all.

I am bak after the general rehearsal of "Marta." Was really a triumph. People was in prevention because they thought to be before an old singer and an old man whom have finisched in voice and in streinght.

What disappointment!! Everybody was crazy. Strow hat and cane come on the stage after my first duet with the baritone and after every song was a veritable delirium.

Here the general opinion was against me because, when an impresario was impossibilated to engage me when the public wish to have me, said that Caruso was over. But when the public come with such prevention and find something also, go crazy. That was the effect of tonight.

The succes is arrived and I hope to send you a cable day after tomorrow in conferming the verdict of the public because tonight was the verdict of the press. It is understood that in the middle of my succes, I dont forget two loves, sweet and darling.

One time I thought always to my mother when I beginning to sing but now, I think at my Doro and my Gloria, my two only thought for whom I must live and to whom I must give my life.

Doro mine! Ah, yes! You are my own heart and the day which for a moment you stop to go in thinking of me I will die.

Your
Rico.

Hotel Sevilla, Havana, Cuba.

13 May 1920. 9 p.m.

My dearest Doro:

　　　　. . . At lunch Bracale come and asked to talk with me. We came up and we talk from 3 p. m. until 7. He want prolonge the season until the 7 of July and go to Porto Rico, Peru, Venezuela. Soon you receive this letter, send me a telegram that for your tranquility you need me near you, otherwise you will be seek because you dont support all the responsibility of the family. Something like that to show Bracale and I am sure he will let me alone. . . .

　　My debut. At nine o'clock last night the performance of "Marta" begin. The first scene of the first act near without any applaudissment. There was Barrientos singing and being tratted like that! I resume that the public wait for me. The second scene beginning and I went out. A great ovation for me for nearly five minutes. I start to sing and I sing very well the first part of the duet with the baritone. There was an applausee contrastato. At the end of the duet finisched with two beautiful haig note. We had a good applause but not so generous and at the end of the act only two calls nearly with protestation. There was many people on the stage with face not very satisfactory. We beginning the second act and all the quartetts passed inobservted, but in the duet I went crazy and took my public. I forget that there was a lady singing with me and I transport with me everybody, maestro, orchestra, Barrientos, and for consequence, the public. I was obliged to come out at open scene five time. Next was the nocturne, "Dormi pur ma il mio riposo," and I sang this very beautifully. We cut the trio between the two ladys and Sir Tristano and for consequence the courtin came down after the ensemble of the nocturne and precisely when Plunket push me in our room. There was seven calls and good clap.

Third act. My romance, beautiful, and ask for encore. Nothing doing. Many calls, but there was somebody which intentionately make SCH! SCH! but was stopped by the public in general. The rest of the opera went well.

At performance over I had many people in my room to compliment me and this morning, as I cabled you, the press was alright. Only the Spanish papers said few words, because for they not exist tenor better than Lazaro, and this was another reason to let the Spanish people in the theatre make discussion about me and this Lazaro.

I dont care because I am sure that little later even the Spanish will agree with me.

I go to sleep. I wish you here!

Your own
Rico.

Hotel Sevilla Havana Cuba

May 14 1920 7 p.m.

My Doro sweetheart:

It is very hot here, but everything is very cold around me. Why? I will tell you. I was accostumated with somebody who was near me all the time, and make the atmosphere full of sweetness and gladness. There was the moment when I steel a kiss with afraid of somebody who dont exist! There was a door which open slowly and a beautiful face came through and say, "I am here." Now all these things are far away from me, and my life is like a piece of meat in the ice-box.

I have very hard time with all the people around me and I dont see how I can get over. They are so stupid and at same time noughty. More I do, more they serve me bad. Punzo is the limit! He try to put Mario in bad light with me and there is fight every moment between everybody, included myself.

It seams that God give me lots of patience to support everyone of this people. The only moment which I am quite is when I am here to write to you, or when I am enclosed in the bath.

Nevermaind! We born for working and for suffrence, and we must took the life as God send to us.

I think is the weather which is so bad, storm, and raining with lots lightning and tunner. Mario have pain in the hand. Zirato in diet, and Fucito also with his head. Punzo live in his ignorency, and so this is the life which we go on and you can imagine how I feel!

My people, perhaps on the bottom of the heart, are not bad, but they dont want any remark. For exemple, last night I made some mistake in the duet with Dulcamara; mistake that was easy to put me at the place if Fucito were attentif. I make the remark and he answer in a way not convenient. At the end of the opera I realize the matter and said something against him. He was not in the dressing-room but Mario and Punzo was there. I dont think that Mario reported what I said but must be Punzo and the consequence was that this morning I had a discussion with Fucito and this thing nearly everyday happens.

But the season of Havana must finish and then everybody his own way.

Oh, my only! If you immagine how I miss you, you will forget everything in the world, even our sweet Gloria! I try to find how I can stop to sing and go near my adorable ones. I hope then, something will happen because I cannot support any more such a life.

> Your
> Rico.

I hope the coming of Mimmi dont truble you—tell him to be a gentleman and not a boy.

Hotel Sevilla Havana Cuba
May 16 1920 11.30 p.m.

Sweetheart Doro my own:

Before I go to bed I wish to send you few words because my heart bitting so strong for my love.

Dont forget to send me a cable in telling me that you need for me because here is the rappresentant of the President of the Republic of Venezuela who are around me to bring me down there.

... Before I was going to the theatre I received your letter of the seven and your cable with which you announce your departure from N.Y. The letter was so sweet that you give me good umor. I saw you in my immagination going up and down from the stears, giving orders, put things on place, talking about food ecc. and I lived with you for some moments. I called you many time: "Doro, where are you?" and I heard in my ears your sweet voice saying, "I am here, my Rico! I am near you, sweetheart, and wish you all good for tonight."

I went to the theatre in good spirit thanks to you. At nine p.m. the performance begin.

My impression was that the people whom heard me for the first time was not satisfied. In effect, they came in with bed intention because they said, "Hear Caruso, in a small opera, (they call 'Martha' small opera before, but not after) and Barrientos without voice, and pay lots money. Is not fair." And for that, sometime during the performance was somebody who do the SCH! SCH!

Must stop now because Bracale come. Until tomorrow.

Your own
Rico.

174

My Big Piece of Gold:

Your letter of the 12th wrote me from New York just arrived and my humor changed at once.

Oh, My Doro! You dont know how I love you! I cry because I cannot stand to be any more far away from you. I wish to have you near me. I am so sad. Dearest, I am crying. I am poor, poor without my Doro. I cant stay anymore far away from you, sweetheart. Let me come near you soon, my own Doro. I feel so miserably! I think I will die here! People are so bad, so unkind! I cannot resist! Oh, my, my Doro! Why I left you? Why I had the bad idea to come here? Your Rico is so down of spirit!

. . . Forgive me for my little breaking! I need it because I felt just like a swelled cloud before a storm! This breaking make me good and I hope you will forgive me to have troubled you. After all, it is a little foult of yourself because you told me many nice things in your letter and that make me cry! You are a witch and I am weak but you know how to take me!

You know I cannot reed your sweetness because you make me feel so emotionated that I start to cry again! I reed you and skratce my head because it seams that all my breans want to go out and show to you that is full of you. My heart jomping so strong for you and when I think about you, he go so quick and hurt me. To let him quite I soon go to kiss your picture with Gloria and he slowly, slowly go to regular muvement.

Ah, dearest, if you be here you will be crazy and not so proud because the injustice will make you furious. We will try to forget as I will forget for the rest of the time that I will be here how to sing, because this people dont understand singing but that only long screams!

Well, I must be calm and I will win.

Kiss for me thousand times Gloria and tell her to not forget her dear Daddy.

To you, my sweet soul, all my love and my thoughts for eternity.

> Your own forever
> Rico

Hotel Seville, Havana, Cuba
May 17 1920 3.30 p.m.

My sweet Doro:

I win another battle with my second performance of "Martha." I took the public by the—what you call the lower part of the mouth, "il mento," (chin) and shake terribly until he came down at my feet.

Here the opinions about me are so dispareted that I dont know who I must content. One day a newspaper say a good thinks and in the same day say bad thinks.

In the two performances which I sing here I try to do my best in giving all my soul and receiving a big dimostration in and out the theatre but this was not enough to conving this savias [wise-acres]!

Yesterday, no, this morning, a news paper said that I was a splended and unic in my second performance, and in the edition of this afternoon said that I am finisched and if I have a succes this is because I have experience of my long carrier and know how to sing. It is stupid and maligno because if I sing well, this is a consequence of my carrier. The people who had not carrier, or school, certenly, dont sing well.

People say to me to laugh but this hurt me and I am afraid to not finisch my performances. I hope one day to weak up and be crazy, in this way I will take the train or the boat and go bak to my dearests. I understand all this thinks. Here are the Spanish whom dont admit that any body also must be great of them but, if I dont loose my mind, I will win in the end.

Tomorrow we go with "Elisir" and if they will not be satisfaiy, I will go away from this hot place. All my love, sweetheart.

Rico.

Hotel Sevilla Havana Cuba
May 18 1920 3 p.m.

My Doro sweetheart:

Nice day today! Eighteen! The day of Gloria nostra! Today she has five months. I hope God will keep her for our affections. We will devote ourself to her in kipping her in good humor and bringing her up sweetly and nicely.

Then she look like me? I dont like because I am offly ogly and always I told to you with the hope to made another yourself! The interesting is that she took your sweetness and this is the most important.

Oh, my own Doro! I adore you both terribly! You can immagine how big must be my love for you because my life was
always troubled for things that was not mine! You are mine, with
Gloria and you give me all the joy and all the happiness of the
life, for consequence I love you both over everything in the
world, and from the moment which I married you, I am yours
and you bring me only glad.

Your

Rico

Hotel Seville, Habana, Cuba.

May 19 1920 2.30 p.m.

My Doro darling:

Now, as I told you in my precedent letter, that I
felt very well for "Elisir," thanks to your three cables. My voice
was fine. I begin the performance very nicely and at the middle
of the duet, like Mexico, I took the public by the chin and at
the end of the first act the callings were immumberably. The
second act I amuse the public and they enjoy very nicely. Many
callings at the end. Third act. Few callings after the duet with
the baritone. Then came the romanza. I never see such things! It
was a storm of clappings. They call tremendously for encore, but
that was my revence to refuse and at the end of the opera there
was a big dimostration.

My sweetheart, to arrive to that, you cannot immagine the
work which I was obliged to doo. The public here dont care if

the other artists sing well or not, if the orchestra dont play well, if the corus sing half toon low, or if the stage is not well arrenged. They wait for me and pend from my lips.

Fortunately, I was in good voice and good spirit and I win the battle.

Now the difficulty is passed because here the "Elisir" and "Martha" was unknow and from now on I will make this people go crazy with all the opera which I go to sing next.

Bracale is here now, and he talking about Lima (Peru), Venezuela, Porto Rico and other towns and country, and I am afraid he will take all my time, because you immagine how much the impresarii talking to convince the artist, for consequence I am sorry I must leave you and I will continue tomorrow.

My darling, I wish you here to see in what conditions I am. I prespire from the top of my head right down to my feet and the wather in coming down make a round around me. Where I toch with my foot the floor, I hear a noise like CIAK! CIAK! My, what a heat!

Doro mine, I am tired and go to bed. You will forgive me if I do not write for any long. Thank you, dearest.

Kiss for me Gloria. To you my soul,

Rico

May 22, 1922 4:30 p.m.

My Doro darling:

Bracale propose me to make a tour in Venezuela and Lima (Peru). After I finish my engagement here I will go to New Orleans and Atlantic City. From there with all your trunks and baby things, take the boat and altogether will go to Porto Rico from when the tour will beguinning, and finish at Lima, Peru. I have no volonty becasue I am tired to sing, and I not yet enjoy of my two Pushinas, you and Gloria. For consequence, if you like to travel with maid, nurse and baby, outside of nervous husband you will cable me and tell me to accept, otherwise cable the reason about the baby, cannot accept that you and she travelling, and you as wife don't allow me to go alone. Do you understand? I like to refuse two hundred thousand dollars because I wish to enjoy my vagation with you, my sweet Doro!

Ah, people here beguin to change idea about me and talking very well. Hope have big success tonight.

I kiss you thousand time with Gloria and in one big hug I tight you both on my heart.

Your

Rico.

My own Doro darling:

As usual we begin the performance of "Ballo Masque" at 9 p.m. and my first song was an esemple of "bel canto" but misunderstand and there was few clappings and at the end of the act two courtin call. At the second act a tremendous ovation to Besanzoni for her "Graves" which the intelligent do not like. My first trio with Besanzoni and Madam Escobar, a Mexican singer, nearly pass under silence. Then came the second part of the same act (II) which is all for the tenor and there I had my ovation with my barcarola and at the scherzo. At the end of the act many courtin call. Third act I had a duet and a terzet. I sung frases in the duet splendedly, and I thought that at the end there will be a tremendous ovation, but by a high note of Madam Escobar, there was no applause. The terzet went well but no clapping. Many courtin call.

First part of the last act I have a big frase in which I give all my soul and there was another ovation. The second part went well, courtin calls at the end of the opera.

But what work for me! You know, my dear Doro, how particular I am in everythings because I like order and let things go nicely, but here it seams that every one works for his own, and for consequence, even with lots rehearsel, nothing goes right. You must know that I like to sing well what the other artists sing without any feeling and for consequence being, orchestra, corus and conductor accostumated to not give any importance, they go on, and this make me nervous and let me loose my feeling. Of course the public remark this things and they apprecie my work. Another work for me is to fight with, not only with the public, but with the compagnons and specially the baritons who want to take the place of the tenor.

In such small companie there are always truble because where I am everybody want have the same succes of me and to arrive to that they try to do things not kind.

Immagine what I know last night. A tenor who was at Metropolitan and try to do bad things to me, said that if I am at Metropolitan it is because the Black Hand help me and dont let take my place from another tenor, and in exchange, I pay nearly all my money to this people of the Black Hand!

From that I immagine how big I am and you consider how I must work to keep my position as cleer as ever.

I find your cable with you beg me to not go to Venezuella and I thank you for it. Bracale is on the thorns waiting your answer. He will go crazy because being the impresario of all this little South American Republics they will be all against him because they say, "You brought Caruso to Cuba and not here. Why?" For consequence he will loose all this places. I do not care because I must care for my dearest wife and my sweet girl and a little for my healt too. I will fight terribly and I will win.

How are you, sweetheart? How is our Gloria of gold? Hope well.

> My own own!
> Rico

Hotel Sevilla Cuba
May 25 1920 6.p.m.

My own Doro darling:

I have your letter of the 20th and this beguinning so cold—only "darling."

Poor my Doro! Ah, the servants are the truble of the life!

Brava! Are not enough the truble, that you find time to study
French? Have you the intention to go in French country? Well,
if this is your pleasure, allright.

Nothing interesting about me—only that tonight I will sing
"Pagliacci."

3 a/m.

Here something about the performance. I was beguinning in
very bad conditions because when things dont go well I loose my
temper and my voice suffre. But at the arioso I closed my eyes,
and I gat everybody with me, public and stage people. What
manifestations, dearest! The stage was coverd with flowers, and
lots of little objects—fan, artificial flowers, straw hats, handkerchiefs and programs. The curtain callings was innummerable and
I was nearly obliged to talk. But I was not able to do, and the
public was glad seeing my lips say, "Muchas gracias, muchas
gracias" and they was satisfied.

Goodnight, dearest. I send you my love and my heart.

Your

Rico

Hotel Sevilla, Havana, Cuba.
Thursday May 27 1920 6.30 p.m.

My Doro sweetheart:

First of all, I must tell you that the critics on "Pagliacci" was all splended. They says that this was the succes of Bracale, because only "Pagliacci" with Caruso is enough for the season. Not bad, and everybody is crazy about.

Of course I work hardly with rehersal and tomorrow we go with "Tosca" which will be a great succes—I hope.

You tell me that you feel rested and the house going beautifully. Poor my Doro! I think never you work like that. Well, that is life. But I am worried for you. Take care, my sweetheart, of your dear self.

I will enjoy, dearest, in everything that you enjoy but remember that I works and my work is so hard that need compensation sometime in the family.

I am fighting here with my work and I hope to go to the end vittoriously even dead, and come back to you with palm and laurel.

You immagine from my caracter what big things happen to make me cry.

Thanks, dear, for all your nice and sweet words. They are like honey that goes in all my blood and give me this quitness that so much I need.

I kiss you with all my affections.

As ever your
Rico

Hotel Sevilla, Havana, Cuba.
May 28th 1920. 3 p.m.

My Doro Darling:

Since I am here I never had such a terrible day! I do not know what is the matter with me! I am so nervous! I dont feel to doo anything, I dont want to see anybody! Everything boder me so! I trat everybody with a bad manners! I think it is the weather because she is clouded and the hot is suffocating. I am tired to stay here! I wish to go away and be near my Doro darling. I am home seek! Here is so noise and I cannot have a moment of quite rest. Autos, tramways, trollys and talking machines makes terrible noise, that my mind go over terribly. Immagine that is a continual play of auto horn, one have not stop than another beginning, at that all day and night! You can immagine my nervs.

I will sing tonight "Tosca," and if my nervs dont go quite, you can immagine the succes. Hope until tonight everything will be alright and specially if I will receive some news from you, because until now, nothing came.

5 p.m.

I am yelling like a crazy, Hurra! Hurra! because I have here before me, three dearest and sweet letters of you! You make my senses all go out of place and from my cold and sentimental temperament you made of me a volcanic sensitive!

If you go around and crying for me, I go around and, like a cat, which feel the earthquake coming and make MEAW! MEAW!

Your
Rico

Hotel Sevilla, Habana, Cuba.

May 29th 1920. 2.20 a.m.

My Doro sweetheart:

Here I am all alone after my performance of "Tosca," and my supper.

I start my performance in good spirit, and my first aria was sang beautifully and the public applauded me enthusiastically. The duet with Tosco, which was never sang in a good way here, because the tenors in every place reserved themself for the arias, was very appreciated and applauded.

In the second act, you know I have so little to doo but this little was appreciated. The third act was the high point of the night. My aria, "E lucevan le stelle" was tremendously applauded with demand of an encore, but I continue to cry and the music went on with a noise of the public.

The rest of the act went very well and at every frases sang by me there was approvation by the public. The result was that everybody says that never before they heard "Tosca" but only the romance of the third act by the tenor, because they only (the public) know that.

The Cubans who heard me in New York says that never I sang better. This is 27th year that the people says that. (Modesty a part.) I have win another victory and I hope to conquist at the end all the country.

Goodnight because I am tired.

A kiss. Near you I want to die.

Rico

My dearest Doro Sweetheart:

. . . I went to the theatre and show your cable to Bracale. He was nearly fainting down. He told me that he will come to New York with me and implore you to accept the proposition because, he said, we cannot throw out from the window two hundred thousand dollars. I try my best to calm him, and I think now he is calm and put his soul in peace.

Then I went in my dressing-room to prepare myself for "Pagliacci." I was so nervous that you cannot immagine. But what a "Pagliacci" I sung! Surprised myself and everybody was crazy! I never see people crying like in such performance.

Of his last performances he wrote:

La Forza del Destino: . . . At the moment which I throw down the pistol, at the end of the first act, the people inside of the stage dont shot and I make a big noise with my mouth like this, BUUUUM!!!! and I kill the father of Leonora! You can immagine the public how laughing! That assure the succes of the night, because the public put himself in good humor because saw me laughing. My aria was sung by your Rico very, very well and there was a big and long applause. Where I was obliged to go out at open scene to thank the public, was after the duet when I am laying down. Six time I was obliged to go out, even wounded!

You must see the face of Stracciari the Baritono after every duet which he sang with me, and always out of key! He was very obseded because the public show him that they dont like the way which he sang.

Carmen: . . . But where I made everybody crazy was at fourth act, the big duet, I do not know myself where I find all this power of voice and drammaticity. I think this came from my brains in which is the motto, "Before you will kill me, I will kill you," and, for consequence I put all my soul in what I doo.

The calls was innumerables. I was obliged to talk and say, "Desculpame, tengo mucha hambre y los applausos que v.s. me prodigan non me sotisfan por esto ve mego de ir a la cama." This means, "Excuse me, I feel so hungry and your applause which is so kindly you are giving to me doesnt fool up my stomac, for consequence I beg you to go to bed!"

. . . You know dearest if you make me happy in our 21st month of marriage? Gloria! You coronated my glory in give me the real one! My Gloria! Then you made me more than happy! You complited the happiness of my new life!

I kiss you and Gloria softly.

Your own
Rico

Chapter Nine

ENRICO had been away six weeks. We decided that the Biltmore was too far from the Metropolitan and, after considering several other hotels, I finally reserved an apartment at the Vanderbilt, on Thirty-fourth Street and Park Avenue.

When the arrangements had been completed I went back to Easthampton. As we would surely accept some invitations when Enrico returned, I decided to take my jewels with me. I carried them in a "keep-safe" that weighed forty pounds and contained an electric gong which, when the alarm was set off, would ring for forty-eight hours. The jewels were in separate cases, except for a diamond comb and a pair of diamond earrings. I placed the safe on the mantelpiece opposite my bed, set the alarm, locked the safe and hid the key.

Spring was late that year—the days were cold and overcast and there was a heavy thunderstorm nearly every night. One evening my brother, his wife and I were sitting in the living room after dinner when a storm of unusual violence broke upon us and the electric lights went out. Frank the butler, who had been Enrico's waiter for years at the Knickerbocker, lighted candles in the brass candlesticks on the mantelpiece. Each crash of thunder rattled the casement windows and torrents of rain rippled the diamond panes.

Then into this very appropriate setting and weather appeared characters and a plot right out of the pages of Nick Carter. It all began by a sharp ring of the doorbell and Frank announcing that Fitzgerald would like to speak to me.

He came in with streams of water running down his black rubber coat. "There's a yellow taxi from New York at the entrance gate," he said, "with a man and a woman who say they want to see Mr. Caruso."

"Who are they?"

"I don't know, but they look queer. He has a cap like a French officer's and she's got on an evening dress. Foreigners."

"Bring them here," I said, "and when they're inside watch them through the window. Frank, don't leave the room after you've announced them."

We were all standing with our backs to the fire when Frank brought them in. I had never seen either of them before. Fitz was right, they did look queer. The man was tall, blond, sharp-featured, unsmiling, and was dressed in an officer's uniform—patent-leather boots, blue breeches with a red stripe, a dark blue tunic and many decorations. The cap he held in his hand was red and braided with gold. A long military cape hung over his shoulder. The woman, older than he, was short and dark. She wore a black taffeta evening dress, a light scarf and a tulle theater hat. Before I could greet them he began to speak.

"I have come to see Mr. Caruso." His English had a strong accent that I couldn't identify. "We must see him immediately."

"Mr. Caruso isn't here," I said, "he is in——"

Frank quickly interrupted me. "Mr. Caruso is in South America—Buenos Aires." I said nothing. Frank knew as well as I did that Enrico was in Havana.

The officer frowned. "But I know he is here, they told me so at the Knickerbocker. We went there at once when we arrived from Europe this morning. Of course he is here."

"He is not here," my brother repeated. "You have heard Mrs. Caruso say so."

"Mrs. Caruso? There is no Mrs. Caruso."

I said, "I beg your pardon, I am Mrs. Caruso."

190

His face flushed and he spoke to the woman in a language I had never heard before. The effect of his words on her startled us—her face turned dark red and she answered him in a voice filled with fury. It grew louder and louder, interrupted by shrieks of laughter and wild sobs. The man didn't attempt to calm her, merely spoke a few words in her direction as he continued to stare at me.

Suddenly his right arm disappeared under his cape. At the same moment my brother seized one of the heavy brass candlesticks. Simultaneously the casement window flew open and Fitz's hand stretched into the room, pointing a revolver.

"Put up your hands and drop your cape!" he ordered.

The man swung around toward Fitz. He tried to laugh as his cape fell to the floor. He took a wallet out of his pocket, extracted a card and tossed it on the table while the woman covered her face with her hands. "I beg your pardon, madame," he said, "there has been a mistake. Here is my card."

Frank brought it to me and I read: Mihail Cattinas, Secretary of the Rumanian Legation, Washington, D.C. In the corner in pencil was written: Hotel Biltmore.

"Madame, will you be so kind as to allow us to remain here for the night? The storm——"

Fitzgerald called through the window, "There is an inn three miles down the road."

The man ignored Fitz and continued to look at me. "We are strangers and we beg your hospitality. You wouldn't put a dog out on a night like this."

"Three miles away, no rooms here," Fitz repeated.

The woman stamped her foot, screamed and rushed from the room. The man made me a deep bow, then turned and followed her. I immediately went to the telephone and called the Biltmore. The manager said that two people answering my description had been there for several days, but had left that morning without paying their bill. Next I called the Rumanian Legation in Washington. There was no one of that name on their staff.

That night I wrote the whole incredible story to Enrico.

Hotel Sevilla Havana Cuba
Tuesday June 1 1920 4.30 p.m.

My dearest Doro:

You cannot imaggine how I suffred in reading your letter with which you describe me the Cattina's visit! Fortunately nothing happens. This people was neither my friends, neither acquaintence because I never heard such a name in my life. I dont make any mistake in saying that this people not came there at such hours in the night for such purpose which they said but, there must be another reason, because when Frank told them I was not at home, was not necessity to be excited. I do not know any Roumanian who is called Cattinas, and the few I know never give sign of life to me. The nationality, the uniform of the man, the refusal to tell you what they want, show to me many bad things. Perhaps they were Roumanians but you must know that this people are all strong people, and when a husband accompagne his wife at some place, as this man did, is always him that must talk before and introduce himself. They NOT husband and wife, but, I am sure, they was a regular crooks and they come with bad intention, beliving to find you all alone.

I am so exciting and I hope you will not see anymore anyone during the night. Give the order to the gate that after the sun is down you dont see nobody. If you have a friend who come in the night give to the gate a pass-word or the name.

But you must not let pass this incident without giving to the

192

Police of Easthampton. I cannot immagine what they want from me, and be so nervous when they dont find me at home. It is strange and misteriously! If people come to see me for business they dont goes crazy when they dont find me and they say the reason of the coming.

If people come for money they dont spend two hundred dollars for a taxi but they write a long story.

If they come to blackmail me there is nothing on me to be blackmailed. I had nothing to do with any Roumanian of kind.

My mind worls about but dont find anything right but all wrong. Take care, my Sweetheart, I am so afraid for you and our Gloria. Look out on everything! Ah, my God! Why I left you?

I have an idea, perhaps to be descarted, but it is better you know. Sometime around big or rich people are parasites that when they see that they beguinning loose ground, and to show that they are necessary, they commit many kind of wrong things just to arrive to have again the faith of the people whom was nearly discontented. I means that: It is many time that Fitz was scolded by me and by you and it is very easy that he arrange this business just to show you his fidelity. Perhaps I am wrong but we have the right to think on everybody and everything.

Do you think that Gloria will caress me when I will be back? I hope so, and if not, I will caress her.

I am ever your
Rico

* * *

Like all people in the public eye, Enrico received many anonymous letters. These increased after our marriage and I had promised to tell him if I received any while he was away. He had asked me not to destroy them but to put them aside for his return. In 1910 the "Black Hand" had sent him a letter demanding fifteen thousand dollars. He took it to the police, who assigned a detective to follow him everywhere. A week later he received a second letter ordering him to leave the money on the front steps of a house in Brooklyn. The police prepared a package and Enrico went to deliver it. The house was surrounded by detectives and when two men came for the package they were arrested. They were convicted and sentenced to seven years in Sing Sing. A year later Enrico added his name to a petition for their pardon.

The anonymous letters we received were generally maligning, insane or pornographic. Enrico had a theory about them: "Watch the first person who comes to see us after such a bad letter, because sometime it could be written by a friend who will wish to see the effect." On at least two occasions he was right—once it was a poor man he had helped with money and once it was a well-known maestro. Each had come to see us unexpectedly, early in the morning. Enrico's sympathetic manner had so melted them that both had broken down and confessed.

"But what made them write to us like that?" I asked. "Because they have bad hearts and they are jealous—one of my money, the other of my name." It wasn't hard to understand why my poor Rico didn't always believe in the sincerity of his friends.

* * *

At Easthampton I prepared the workroom for his return, where he could paste his clippings and I could arrange the stamp collection. This room could be entered either from my bedroom or by the outside staircase. A bolted screen door made it safe to leave the heavy wooden door open at night.

194

I was sitting in the library one evening, working on a tapestry for Enrico. My brother had gone to New York, but his wife sat sewing beside me. At nine o'clock I went upstairs to look at Gloria and say goodnight to Nanny, then returned to my embroidery. Half an hour later I glanced out the window and said, "There's no moon tonight." At that moment I heard the violent ringing of the alarm bell in the safe from my bedroom above.

I flew from the library and ran across the hall toward the telephone in the pantry. Enrichetta came running down the stairs, screaming, "Your pearls!" I shook her and told her to stop shrieking. I could hear the bell of the safe ringing in the distance as I called police headquarters. The sergeant asked me to describe the jewels and as I talked I could hear him giving orders to stop all cars on the roads to New York. By now the servants were gathered outside the pantry door. Frank wanted to pursue the burglars, but I forbade anyone to leave the house, reminding them that we were unarmed and that men who would steal such valuable jewels would kill to keep them. Only Fitz had a revolver, and when his telephone at the cottage didn't answer I called the local police and the sheriff. As I left the telephone Fitz came in the front door. He knew nothing of what had happened and had met no one on the road to the house. He drew his revolver and we ran upstairs. Gloria and the children were safe in their beds and had not even wakened.

The only evidence of burglars was my empty mantelpiece and a slit of four inches in the wire of the screen door leading to the outside stairs, wide enough for a hand to have passed through and reached the bolt. In the distance the alarm bell was still ringing, and Fitz started out in the direction of the sound. Twenty minutes later he came back, carrying the open safe, which he had found in a clearing. All the cases of jewels were gone, but he had picked up the diamond comb and earrings from the grass. Not only Fitz but everyone else in the house had handled the safe by the time I thought of fingerprints.

Although I telegraphed to Enrico immediately, he had already heard the news from the Associated Press. In the morning I had a cable from him: "Thanks God you and baby are safe. Will replace jewels."

Hotel Sevilla Havana Cuba
Wednesday June 9 1920 4 a.m.

My dear Doro:

I do not know what I go to write to you because my head are turning like a motion perpetuo!

The news which I received tonight (I mean this morning) about the robbery make me so excited and nervous that you cannot immagine.

I had to fight with my performance of "Aida" because I do not know what the public want of me, but I win in every respect and I had a big dimonstration. I remark that during the performance the people who were accostumated to smile at me and congratulate me, was very black, and I thought that was in account of my singing, which was better than ever. That made me crazy and I said to Bracale that I will go away because here is not place for me. Poor man! He knows the business and he dont say anything but he change of color and goes away.

After the performance we was at the table in the dining-room for supper. There was about two o'clock and at the beguinning of the supper a waiter come with a card for Zirato. I dont know if was feeling, or what, I asked to Zirato who send a card at two o'clock in the morning. He was unable to talk and I thought was

196

something bad, as you know I think always bad to have the good. He says, "I will tell you after," and he get up and goes out.

I asked to Fucito and Stefanini of Mexico, who is here, and somebody else but nobody answer me.

I understand something was wrong and when Zirato camed back I impose on him who send the card. Then he give me a telegram that the Associated Press sent around the world.

This telegram said, "The country home of Enrico Caruso tenor was burglarized this afternoon and jewels valued at $500,000 were stolen, the police reported tonight. The stolen jewels included a pearl necklace valued at $75,000."

You can immagine where goes my supper and how my blood became! Quick I thought at the Cattinas and this are the one which made the business. They arrived to the larder as a cat!

Then I went to the cable offices and the first thing I doit was to ask if there was a cable for me. "Yes, two," said the employers. They gave to me and was this two: "Dont worry. We are all safe. All police of Long Island and New York watching every road, bridge, and train. Everything being done that can be done. Have given description of cook and kitchen-boy and Cattinas. House full policemen. Dont be frightened. Doro." (Not a kiss!)

I sent another cable with a adjoint like this: "I dont care for robbery but wished you had informed me about your and Gloria's health. Lots jewels will come. Hope nobody hurt and amire all in the house that they have my confidence."

My head hurt me! I am crying for the pain which arrived suddenly and so strong!

I dont understand how happen this business. You are there 12 *people, and nobody was at home? This means lightness from somebody. Think if they had stoled Gloria!!*

I dont want say anything else but I wait for the evenements.

I kiss you and Gloria, both my dearests, with my as ever affections,

    Your

    Rico

P.S. It is funny that Fitz in coming back home dont see the burglar, but find the box after was robbed. Where was his wife at the moment of robber? Where the dogs stop to smell footsteps?

Three different companies had insured the jewels, and by noon the next day ten detectives were living in the guesthouse. They searched every inch of the grounds, dragged the lake and questioned each member of the household over and over again. The publicity became enormous and unescapable. Fortunetellers began to arrive by train and taxi and so many reporters appeared that I turned the tennis court into a press room. Our mail had to be delivered in bushel baskets—there were literally thousands of letters from cranks; I wouldn't have believed there were so many lunatics in the city of New York. People telephoned so continuously to give advice and warnings that in desperation I sent for my lawyer to come and live in the house and take charge of the chaos. He brought in a handwriting expert to open all the mail. Every day early in the morning cars full of investigators arrived from the offices of the district attorney, the sheriff and the local police.

For the next three weeks I lunched and dined with my ten detective guests, listening to tales of crime and murder. Some of the detectives were Irish, some were Italian, and in addition to racial competition they were pitted against each other in the even greater struggle for the large reward offered by the insurance companies. They tiptoed through the house in the dead of night, sneaked about the grounds with drawn revolvers and as a climax claimed to hear Sicilian whistles in the woods. This alarmed me. I engaged a special detective—a sympathetic Italian—to guard Gloria.

Five nights after the robbery a reporter from the United Press telephoned me: "We have just received word that a bomb was thrown tonight on the stage of the opera house in Havana during the first act of Aïda. We don't know whether Mr. Caruso was injured or not."

All that night I sat by the baby's bed, praying. The next morning a cable came from Enrico telling me that he was safe.

From the house of Mr. and Mrs. De Berenguer, Santa Clara, Cuba
16th June 1920 Noon.

My Sweetheart:

> *Now I will give you some information about the bomb. "Aida" begins nearly three quarters of an hour late. I goes out and sing my romance, Celeste Aida, very well, and everything goes well until the end of the first act (temple scene). The second scene beguinning with the scene of Amneris and Aida, then come the scene of the triumphe of Radames. But this scene dont had the time for beguinning because at the end of the duet of the two woman, there was a big explosion.*

> *I was in my dressing room to fix my mantle and I nearly put a pin in my shoulder because I was sposted [thrown down] by the force of the air caused by the explosion. Then I see the people in the corridor of the dressing rooms run away and in their faces they had the expression of terror!*

CARUSO AS RADAMES IN *Aïda*

Somebody told me, "Go away because there will be some other explosions." I was very calm and quick I ron on the stage, full of pieces of sticks which came down from the scenic arc.

The courtin was down but I went out of it, and there was all the public stand up. Some orchestra people play the National Hymn, and many people talking and gesticulating. The orchestra was full of debris and the side boxes full of dusty. I was tooked away from somebody and accompzagned in my dressing room. Lots people came and everybody said his version. In this moment a man come and said, "Everybody out, because the performance was stopped by the authority and the stage begin to go in fire." He dont said that two time that I, dressed with my best costumes, was in the street, and jomping in a car which was waiting for his owner, went to the hotel and cabled you.

Then, where was the bomb? Who put that down? Why dont explode in the audience against whom was direct? The bomb was put in the water closet of the gallery near the scenic arc and been in this plaster, was very easy to come down. The bomb dont explode in the audience, because there was not the intention. Against who? First thing said, against me. After against Bracale. All this thought are to be descarted, because against me was too late. If was anarchista they must put down the bomb when all the élite of Havana was there the first night. Babars! There were about 30 wounded and fortunately the public went out slowly and nothing happened.

To you, all my soul.

Your

Rico

Chapter Ten

BRACALE kept insisting on the South American tour, and Enrico wrote:

I told him that I have no volonty to work anymore but he insist terribly and I cannot put him at the door. In any case we will see after your answer what will be the attitude of this impresario, and if the matter will be desperately for him, we will see if we can do something. If there will be the possibility, if you say that you can leave baby at home, there will be 14 days of sea to go and 14 to come back. Will be this not too much for you? You know, Bracale is old impresario and he knows how to took the artist like me—with kindness and sommission, and I cannot treat him in bad way, for consequence I am always bodered from morning in the night about propositions of every kind.

After receiving my cable of refusal Enrico wrote again:

Bracale show me your cable! He is nearly died! You had seen the face of this man—he changed in many ways, positions and coulors! He talk for nearly three hours, and he wish to send you another cable, but this time by me, and he will be here tonight for the propos. I dont know what I go to do and I am afraid to have a very hard time.

The next day:

With holy patience I had another long talk with Bracale about Peru. He asked me if I received answer to cable I sent to you but I told him I dont send it and he said, "Good." I was surprised and I ask, "Do you change your mind about to bring me to Lima?" He said "Not at all. I think better dont boder any more Madame with telegram because she will say always no, no, and more no. The best thing to do," he said, "is this. When you goes back you will convince her to come down to Lima with you because I have time to wait. I see," he continue, "you like to come and I am sure you will convince her to come with or without the baby."

I looked him in the eyes and see that he was sincere and I told him my sincerity too, because in that moment my soul cannot lie and approfited of that to tell him what I go to tell you now because that will be for the good of everybody. First I told him, "I will try my best to convince Madame and I am sure that she will come with me" (as I am sure you will when you hear the reasons).

Now dearest, if you see a change in me is because with this money of Lima, I will be covered for two years for the income tax in Italy and in the U.S.A. and if something arrive to me after this season of Lima, we can give a good-by to the theatre and we will be alright without selling any bonds.

Think a little about and you will see that I am alright. If you are afraid about Gloria, I have thought about that and what to do in that case.

I hold you both on my heart.

Your

Rico.

In the end he definitely rejected Bracale's offer, being too apprehensive about our safety to leave us, and convinced by the doctor that the South American climate and food might be harmful to Gloria.

* * *

The Havana season was now over and Enrico was on his way home. He was to stop off at Atlantic City to give a concert and I joined him there with Gloria. When he met us at the station his first words were, "We are safe now," and it wasn't until weeks later that he said, "Doro dearest, don't you think it was a little foolish to leave everything on the fireplace?" "But, Rico, I could always see the safe from my bed." "Ah, I see."

He had brought me a diamond watch and a lump of gold bigger than an egg that had been presented to him by Bracale. On one side was an inscription to commemorate his escape from the bomb, and embedded in the top was a little stone from the wrecked theater.

Mimmi was waiting for us at Easthampton. He had grown taller and was wearing a Boy Scout uniform. "What for you do that?" said Enrico. "You are American soldier?" Mimmi tried to explain, but his father said, "Never mind. You play soldier if you want, but when I was your age I worked." Later that day I told Mimmi that I wanted him to go to the Culver Military Academy in the fall, as the training there would help him when he returned to Italy to do his military service, and I was sure the plan would please his father. Enrico was delighted with it and added that Mimmi shouldn't waste all his time that summer; why not practice the piano and take some lessons from Fucito? I was glad that a little bond had been established between them.

The detectives were still creeping around the house and they so disturbed Enrico that he asked them all to leave, with the exception of our private Italian guard.

My birthday was the sixth of August. It started happily but ended, for me, in terror. At breakfast Enrico said, "We must begin to fill another box," and presented me with a beautiful emerald-cut diamond. We passed the morning fishing for perch off the pier—a new experience for Enrico, who had never fished before. In his excitement he fell into the lake, where he stood waist-deep in water, laughing and shouting for Mario. When Mario came with a bathrobe he also brought the mail, and while Enrico was climbing back on the pier I idly opened the first letter on the pile. It was typewritten and unsigned. In literate and precise English it demanded $50,000. If this sum were not sent within six days to an address which we would find in the personal column of the *Evening Telegram*, Enrico, the baby and I would be killed. The money was to be paid in one-hundred-dollar bills and on no account were we to communicate with the police.

Seeing my face, Enrico took the letter from my hand and read it slowly. Then he said in a calm voice, "Do not be afraid, Doro."

"But what shall we do? Aren't you going to call the police?"

"Better not to speak any more before Mario. Do not tell the servants or Mimmi. But also do not be afraid."

There were six days to be lived through before the twelfth of August. The first three passed in outward calm, with Enrico clipping and pasting as usual. He didn't speak of the letter again, only of the concert he was to give in Ocean Grove on the fourteenth—if we're alive, I thought.

On August 10 Mimmi left to visit friends. Enrico passed the morning of the eleventh selecting the songs for his encores. We lunched alone as usual. The afternoon was hot and sultry.

"I don't feel to work today," he said. "Let us go for a nice drive. Tell Nanny and Gloria to come too. Also the guard—he can sit with Fitz if he wants to take fresh air."

During the drive he laughed and joked with the detective—I wondered if he could have forgotten that tomorrow was the twelfth.

"I think we go back now," he said, after an hour's driving. As we approached a railroad crossing we heard a train coming and stopped to let it pass. But instead of passing, it whistled and stopped too. "All 'right, boss," said our detective, jumping out and opening my door. "What is it?" I asked Enrico. "We go to New York, Doro darling, in this train. We return on the fifteenth after my concert in Ocean Grove." "But baby and Nanny?" "They too. Come get in the train and you will see."

In the train I found Enrichetta and Mario with our luggage. Enrico had made all the arrangements with the detective, without saying a word to anyone. Even the servants didn't know where they were going.

As the train started, Enrico said, "Sorry you were so nervous, my Doro, but it was better so. Your nerves helped to hide my plan. Don't ever again be afraid for the bad letters. I always fix everything for you and the Puschina."

I thought that nothing could ever frighten Enrico after the last two months of bombs, burglars and threats of death, but I was wrong. When we went to Gloria's room that night after the concert-and found her lying upside down between the twin beds, he was beside himself. "She suffocate, my God!" he shouted, hoisting her up by the legs. "She cannot speak—call doctor quick!" He was in a panic. Then Gloria smiled and threw up. "Thank God she lives!" he cried.

Nanny fastened Gloria back in bed with two big safety pins. "What do you mean by frightening your poor father?" she said. "Now you go to bed too, Mr. Caruso, you look a bit worn out."

* * *

Back in Easthampton, we looked forward to a few weeks of rest. This was the first summer Enrico had spent in America, and so far he had had no real holiday. Friends sometimes came to dine and occasionally we lunched with them.

In the middle of August members of the fashionable Southampton summer colony organized their annual fair for the benefit of the local hospital, and Enrico was invited to be their main attraction. They offered him a special booth where he would spend the day making caricatures of all comers at ten dollars each. He accepted with pleasure and as we started off for the fair he said, "This holiday I like. I will make many funny drawing and have a nice time."

A committee met us at the entrance, and we walked through the grounds. Enrico bought boutonnieres from pretty girls, tombola tickets from clamoring boys and stopped at each booth to admire the decorations of bright streamers and flowers.

"Your booth is heavenly, Mr. Caruso," said Mrs. X., who was escorting us. "I know you will adore it." She indicated one, larger than the others. It was hung with red, green and white streamers, two Italian flags and a long thick fringe of dry spaghetti.

Enrico stopped. "What is that?" he asked. The pleasure had gone out of his eyes and his face had become a formal mask. "I am sorry, madame," he said, "but I cannot make my drawings in there. Please have the spaghetti taken down." Then he added with a smile, "Spaghetti, you know, is for the kitchen and I am not yet hungry." The consternated committee immediately substituted other decorations.

On the way home he said a little sadly, "They do not imagine such thing will offend because many people think of Italians only like that. What surprise me is that such nice people make such mistake. Sometimes I feel far away from my old life in Signa."

* * *

Soon Enrico was to start on one of the longest and hardest concert tours he had ever undertaken—in the space of one month he was booked to sing in Montreal, Toronto, Chicago, St. Paul, Denver, Omaha, Tulsa, Fort Worth, Houston, Charlotte and Norfolk.

He had decided to take the apartment I had reserved at the Vanderbilt, and we went to New York for a few days to give final orders. It was on the top floor, with a penthouse, and had been built by Alfred Vanderbilt for his own use. The red brocade walls of the enormous salon made a perfect background for Enrico's antique furniture and vitrines. He at once chose the place for the beautiful medieval credenza—the center of the wall between two high windows; above it would be a marble Madonna which he specially loved, a bas-relief made by the Master of the Madonnas in the fifteenth century.

Enrico spent his last few days in Easthampton rehearsing with Fucito his complete program for the tour. These private concerts, to which I listened in the studio, were surely better than any the public would ever hear. Here, free of the responsibility of audiences and the strain of traveling, Enrico could sing for his own enjoyment and his voice, after a two months' rest, was as fresh as a boy's. He told me an astonishing fact, unknown to the public—that he might have been as successful a basso or baritone as he was a tenor. His great eyebrows moved up and down his forehead as he laughed over the story of how he had once used this gift to save his friend, Andrés de Segurola, at a performance of *Bohème* in Philadelphia. In the train Andrés had become suddenly hoarse and told Enrico he was worried about the evening's performance. There was no understudy for the role of Colline and the loss of his voice would mean a disaster. Enrico advised him to hold back as much as possible for the first three acts and save himself for his big aria, "*Vecchia zimarra*," in the fourth. Although Andrés had agreed, when he went on the stage the idea vanished and from the very beginning he held back nothing at all. Consequently after the third act he stood backstage shaking and as hoarse as a crow. Polacco, who was con-

ANDRÉS DE SEGUROLA AS COLLINE IN *La Bohème*

ducting, knew nothing of the desperate basso's situation and gave the signal for the fourth act to begin. He saw Colline enter with his broad felt hat pulled over his face; watched him bring a chair to the footlights, take off his greatcoat, place his foot on the seat of the chair and sing the famous farewell song to his

209

coat. At the end of the aria there was great applause as Colline left the stage; then Caruso came on as Rodolfo and the act finished as usual.

Hardly had the curtain descended when Polacco rushed to Enrico's dressing room in a rage. "Are you crazy?" he shouted. "If the audience had recognized you as Colline it might have ruined the performance."

"It was a good joke on Polacco," Enrico said. "He did not know I was such a good basso." *

After this tour de force the Victor Company asked Enrico to make a record of the coat aria for their private files. Naturally neither he nor Mr. Child would permit it to be published. "Besides," Enrico beamed, "it would not be fair to the other bassos."

Once he saved another singer, his friend Tetrazzini, in a similiar crisis. She lost her voice just before an important concert and telephoned Enrico for help. He told her to stop at the Knickerbocker on her way to the Hippodrome. She came dressed in white satin spangled in rhinestones and a little ermine cape that fell to her waist. She had masses of bright yellow curls above a chubby smiling face, and she was as round as a ball.

"I can't speak," she whispered, as we led her into Enrico's bathroom. He lifted her up on the edge of the tub, where she sat with her feet resting on a stool, looking like a little pouter pigeon, while he prepared his magic spray—a mixture of ether and iodoform which he always used in emergencies. This medicament was not a cure but had the property of restoring the voice for a period of three hours.

They made a picture I shall always remember—these two great

---

* Geraldine Farrar, who well remembers this incident, says that audiences never notice impromptu changes in the libretto or stage business. "Once when I was singing *Bohème* with Bonci," she added, "he lost his voice. I sang a third of his role for him and the public never knew the difference."

210

artists, one with eyes tightly closed and mouth wide open, repeating "Ah-ah-ah" as she balanced precariously on the edge of the tub; the other, in big spectacles, peering professionally down her throat and puffing a little atomizer with great speed and concentration.

* * *

A fortnight before Enrico left for Canada he went to Camden to make records. At the end of a long day he sang Rossini's *Messe Solennelle*. This was the last record he ever made.

Chapter Eleven

In train from Montreal to Toronto.
Tuesday, Sept. 28 1920. 10 a.m.

My Doro sweetheart:

Here I am, all for you, closed in my drowing room and before I begin to work in something, I let my heart talk to you, my Doro, simpatica, beautiful and good like the bread.

Yes, dearest, I dont expected such a succes being in the condition of cold in which I was. I think that was my low blod pression that not let me nervous and, in effect, I was very calm even without try the voice.

As I said, the succes was tremendous. About ten thousand people inside and out, waited for me, and when I appear on the stage, a big reception was made to me. I was nearly emotionated. I begin to sing my aria from "Bohème" and at the end a tremendous applause broke down. I was forced to give three encores. They want more but I refuse because there were two more numbers to sing.

The public was in good spirit all night and even that had part in the succes.

The second number was the aria of "Elisir d'amore" and even after that three more encores. The aria of "Pagliacci," which I sang better than never was tremendously applauded. The public was all stand up and with programs and handkercifs, saluited me for a long time. No encore after that but many calls, and finally the people after understanding that I dont give any more encores, live the hall.

We went home glad and saying, "Who well begin is half of his work."

Mr Coppicus payed me for this concert 10 thousand dollars in a check, which I sent right away to the Columbia Bank.

It is not funny what happen to us? I mean the things which happened to me arrived the same to you: I dont sleep, you dont sleep! I feel hot, you feel hot! I miss you, you miss me! I explain that as a riciprocity of sentiments and thought!

Since I gat up this morning, after a good night of rest, I give sivere disposition to not allowed anybody came up. My disposition are not observed because some one come in. . . .

2 p.m.

Sorry, dearest to keep you wait for four hours, but you know when I beguin to talk to convince people upon certain point take me long time and here was a long discussion. I make myself tired in this way but I cant help. It was Governess of Mimmi. He wrote me and say that he is studying very hard, but I dont believe. Bad for himself.

I kiss you and Gloria with my heart.

Your
Rico

King Edward Hotel Toronto
Sept 30 1920 11 p.m.

My Doro Sweetheart:

Here I am home after the concert. I have sent you just now a telegram telling you that I dont need anything from Signa and about the concert which went as usual. People little cold from that of Montreal but I was obliged to give one encore more than the last city. Altogether I sing ten songs. I was in good shape but less of feeling because soon I went out to sing my first number I was taken by the steem heat which make me nervous—but—Caruso was there and he respond of his personality.

Now I will have a milk-toast and a little chicken salad and go to bed because I must gat up at 6 a.m. to take the train at 8 o'clock for Chicago.

My succes in Montreal was great but as always there must be somebody whom dont like me. In effect, a newspaper published a critic and not so nice like everyone else. But there are the other newspapers which with their critics answered the one which was not satisfied. Immagine, this said that I, as a concert singer, am lower of Gorgoza and Julia Culp! Bravo the idiot!

All my affectionated love.

From your own
Rico

214

My Doro:

... In this moment we are passing a forest and I see the sun covered of a brown cloud and very strong. I can see the sun, but he is without rays. Very funny effect. I thought was an eclipse.

I think some storm came because in the sky is a big dark brown cloud like a strong smoke, which come to us very quickly.

The train stop now and from my window I see a beautiful picturpiece of green grass—a trak of rail-road which pass through a very thik forest opening a passage and the bekground is bleu. The sky up the tree is pale bleu for only a little space, then the brown cloud, from which the sun red pass through and seams a big water melon.

Now we are in a step, means enormous extencions of ground without trees. Now, funny; all cabbages! Hi! How many cabbages! There are prayries with anucche. Small white houses in wood. What beautiful town—Walley.

The brown clouds, do you guess where come from? From the erth! Yes, they blow from the fields for a big extencion and that make the sky dark.

Now we are in a region of red erth which pass all over. The sun is out now and his color is like bright silver. It seams to see this fire-works which imitates the electricity in the air.

We are dancing in this train very well.

Where are my two Sweethearts? Far! Far! But near because I have both in my heart!

Your

Rico

215

The Saint Paul in Saint Paul.
5 Oct. 1920 8.p.m.

My sweet Doro:

Here I am again with you before I up to bed.

. . . I went to a big club where I was invited to be present, they said, to big meeting for the Community Chest. It is 45 organizations of charity altogather, and they want me as guest of honor. We went with Coppicus and soon I enter in the big hall where the people, about 500, was heating. They got up and salut me with a big applause. I was at the left of the President whom ask me if I prepered the spich." "What spich?" I said. "Well, well," he said, "You see, all this people wait to hear your speek-ing voice and I hope you will please them." You imagine my face! I became first red, then white, then jello and after giv-ing a good score to manager Mr Coppicus, I said, "All right I will talk!" After the lunch, which I dont touched, the President gat up and said after saluting everybody, "Here Mr Caruso will say few words about our meeting." Other salutation and I gat up. Profound Silence. I remarked, before I begin to talk, on the table something printed, and with a smile of satisfaction for myself, because I find a way to gat over this importunity and, as I said, I gat up and said, "Ladis and Gentlement, Mr President. Many thanks for the honor which you all are giving to me with all your manifestation. But I am not here to talk but to sing." At this moment I expect somebody say, "Sing then," but nobody mouve. Then I said, "Do not expect a big spich; I will reed few words that somebody also put before me and save me from this sur-prise!" Than I took the printed paper that was before me and I reed as follow; "I believe in the Community Chest I believe in the plain of giving once for all and enough for all. I believe in the work of the forty five social service agencies in the Community Chest, and that they should be supported, for they are working for the good of all of us. I believe in helping my fellow men!"

You dont imagine, dear, the succes. Nobody expected my presence of mind and the sens of humor. Great applause and after had made lots of caricature.

I love you, my Doro darling! I love you until to disteste you because you took all my heart, and I am so glad for it!

Rico

The Saint Paul in Saint Paul.
Oct. 6 1920. 3 p.m.

My Doro:

Here I am again to you, my own sweetheart, to pass some of my time in your company and let pass from me this little nervous which the blowing of the wind has put in my sistem. Yes, dearest, it is a beautiful day but with the kind of wind which go in the bones.

I had this morning, after making my toilet, some other stupid interview. This newspaper man make me nervous because they ask some foolish question. For exemple, "Wy Caruso let pay the public more of everybody also?" You immagine my face!!! Fortunately Coppicus arrived in time and explain very well the situation. Somebody also ask if I let become My Gloria an acrobata*!!!* I tell you, if was not for such big amount of money which I gat, many time I can send this people to Hell!

P.S. Now about the car. What kind of people are in this garage?

To change the garage because they wash the car with to much soap? I think this is a very poor reason because it is very easy to tell no wash the car with so much soap. There must be some other reason.

I am contented that you improve on the piano and I am sure that in one year you will be able to accompagne me, a little and easy song.

I miss you, and I miss your sweet voice.

Rico

In train from Omaha to Denver
Oct 7 1920 7 p.m.

My dearest Doro:

Before the night become old (nice expression) and my mind become eavy for the tiredness, I am here to pass little time with you, my own darling.

I am tired to be far away from you, and after what happened last night, I feel to not work any more! I will tell you what happened.

After I left you with my last letter of yesterday afternoon, I begin my toilet for the concert. There was a little excitement to close everything on account to leave after. At eight fifteen we begin. First the violin, second the soprano, third me, with "Africana" aria. At home I try my voice and was very good. I begin, than, to sing my aria and the voice respond well at the

218

beginning. There was just not far of ten feet from my head, two lines of electric light which nearly burn my head. So, in singing, I begin to feel for the hot, my respiration very hard and my voice eavy. I felt all my blod going to the head and just at the last hiig note, the blod stop at the throat, and there was a big CRAC which I escaped and went down quickly. I and the public were surprised! I stay a little near the piano because my head was full of blod. Fucito came near me and help me to go down from the platform. There was some applause but not enthusiastically. I went out again for encores but I remarck that I begin well to sing and by the way my head feel very warm. After the first encore I looked this two line of electric light and I saw that this was the cause. I gat little far from the line and sing the second encore. No hot. I tray again to sing at the first position the third encore and there was the same effect. Then the cause of my truble was the light. I went in and give order to pull up this two line of light. They do it. My two others number of the program went alright and the encore too. But there was not enthousiam because myself and public, after this first incident, were very cold. I being careful and the public not being taken for the first song, was always in dout. This was my impression.

We finish the concert at ten, and we rush to the station to take the train which posponed the departure for 20 minutes just to take us on.

I sent Zirato away before to sent you the telegram, and with the death in my heart, I seet down in my drowing room! After a wile Coppicus came with the supper, but I not touch a things. I was, and steel thinking, what the papers will say about.

I think that a man who came to interview me yesterday morning was a "jettatore" [bad luck] because he asked me, "I do not understand how you keep yourself in such good condition for so long and in traveling so much." "Well," I said, "because I take care of myself." And there was the incident in the night must be like that!

I had a very bad night and no sleep at all!

If I tell you something, perhaps you dont beleive me, but I will tell you just the same. Far away from you I have a sentiment of fraidness. I do not know what is this but I feel like a boy without protection. What is this then? Can you explain? At this feeling I add the one of my work and, been far away from you, my life is the most miserable one.

I am beguinning to be old and I am afraif that you will stop to love me. I will kill you, Gloria and myself if that is so!

Your
Rico

Brown Palace Hotel, Denver, Colo.
Oct 9th 1920 11 p.m.

My Doro Sweetheart:

Just finish my concert and have sent you a telegram about. I sung eleven song instead of three before a big, very big audience. They want more, more and more, but in everything have a limit and I think that with eleven song they can be satisfy. A very funny thing is that everybody knows "A Vucchella," and soon the maestro attack the introduction, there is a big applause. My voice was better than in St Paul but I work too much to arrive to have the success. I think was very bad to start the tour with my terrible cold. I feel it in my chester and he will take long time to go away. I hope with the change of temperature will decide to pass away.

Here we are very haigh, three thousand foot of altitude and is very difficult for singer but I went alright. Here the weather is delicious. Hot like plain summer, but breezed by a little wind.

I forget to tell you that the critics of St Paul were very nice. I expect very bad criticism on account of my singing. There was one critic which said that the wires of light trouble me at beguin but when this was pulled up everything was allright.

... I forget to tell you that a man came in with a poesia telling me to give him a chance in putting music on his verses. Poor man—perhaps he dont sleep all night for that. Coppicus put him nicely at the door.

... Navone, our linen store in Florence, surprised me what you tell about. There is always the same story; "Who pay before is always badly served."

Here enclosed you will find two checks, one for $10,000 and one of $7,000 which you will put on your account in the bank as usual.

I envy you in going out and eat nice spaghetti, because is very difficult to have some. Everybody which I meet say, "I wish to give you a nice plate of spaghetti but my cook is in vacation." They let us make water in the mouth and swallow down.

When I will be back we will go all alone in this little restaurant. Yes? We will act as two sweetheart, yes? We will have a drive after and tell each other lots lovely things.

As ever and forever I send to you and Gloria my affectioned thoughts and the kiss that come from the bottom of my heart.

Your

Rico

Hotel Fontenelle Omaha Neb.

Oct 12 1920 11.30 p.m.

My darling Doro:

Just finish my dinner and I want send you my
love and my night kiss. Melon, chicken, patotos, salad, grape jus
and ginger-ale was my dinner.

I have sent you half an hour ago a telegram telling you about
the concert which went magnificaly. Eleven songs, and if I want,
they can accept with pleasure some others but I must take care
because I am not yet over of the cold and I work too much to
arrive to the end.

I told you in my last telegram to send me to Tulsa a blanck
check of the Fifth Ave Bank because I have an idea. We must
be always careful and for consequence I have that idea. Here you
will find a check to you for $100,000 which you will keep until I
arrive home. If something will happen to me you will soon present that check to the Bank to cash. The same you will do when
you will receive the one of the 5th Ave Bank which I will send
you from Tulsa.

I will send to you all my check which Coppicus give me and
you will put this at your account at the bank, in that way we
dont loose the interest. You will forgive me I talk like that but,
dearest, I am traveling and we dont know what will happen.
When I will be home then we will fix the things that we dont
worry anymore because we must think now even for our Gloria.
Why that? Because I love you!

I need you like wather when I am thorsty. I need your voice,
sweet voice, which is so good for my nervs. I need you all around
me.

You are piece of myself, and, being far away from you, I feel something less on my body. Never more out without my two loves! I dont care to work any more and for consequence, is not necessaire to be separated again! I think if I dont work anymore, we have enough to leave and to pay the tax. We will go in my, our, country and we will have good time without be nervous every moment! I am looking for this day! You can immagine how glad I will be when I have not to think about my voice! Hope God let me arrived at such day and then my happiness will be comblet.

I close my eyes and in thinking of you, my own, own heart, am always your own.

Rico.

Hotel Tulsa Tulsa Oklohoma
Oct 16 1920 11.30 p.m.

My Doro:

. . . I meet then Mr Henkel whom present me some gentlemen and some lady whom I dont remember the name. They ask me go to see a mine of oil blowing up. I refused on account of my concert. They insisted in saying that this was thing which not always happened. They said that was question of two hours and we have lunch on the road. I refused again but there was other artists who goes, and finally I accepted.

We arrived after one hour to a town calling Superia and we had lunch—not so bad. I asked how many miles for the fild. They said few more. We leave the lunch-room at two o'clock and gone,

gone, gone and gone. There was four o'clock when we arrived at the fild but in what condition! I never jumped up and hurt myself like that! The road was terrible—we passed two ranches—wilde and orrid place—I was very nervous because I beguin to see that I put the concert in danger.

I hurry up the people to blowing up the mine. We expected to see all the ground around us jumping up like an earthquake. There was lots precaution but at the moment we dont hear any explosion but only six or seven blowing of oil coming up and that is all.

I am under an attack of blod pression. I cannot go on.

All my love

Your Rico

Huckins Hotels Fort Worth Texas

Oct 20 1920 8 p.m.

My Sweetheart:

        I am so sorry but you immagine my condition when I am sure to find you at home, and you was not there! You will forgive me, dearest! I telephoned you again and the girl told me it was 7 p.m. in New York, for consequence I was mad not because you go around to amuse or let pass the time, but because there was some hours that you must be at home. You was at home at that hours but I call you late and the fault was from the girl of the telefone, with whom we must be engry.

You can go out, my dear darling, because I never told you you must dont go out. You know I am like a baby sometime. When a baby think to find something nice at home and dont find, gat mad. So I am. For consequence not be so nervous now. Go out and amuse yourself because is better for you, otherwise you will gat sik.

. . . The concert was the best one of the tour. Six thousand people crazy. My voice were superb and I enjoy myself. After the concert I went to the house of Fay's Sister and ther I meet nearly all the family. The mother is the nice little cute thing I never see. They were so kind with me, and at 4 a.m. I came home.

I had to hear a tenor and a soprano voices, and I were very rude. Yes, people have such nerve to come to me without voice and let me loose my time.

I too, have hard time with newspapers here and especially in this State. The reporters came, ask things and write something else and put me in ridicul in the eyes of the public. For exemple, in Tulsa a reporter ask me if I never been in Texas. I innocently answered, "Are we in Texas?" "Oh, yes, of course we are in Texas!" Then there was the interview published, and in an editorial in the same paper, they criticize me as I never know that there was a State calling Texas. I had the volonty to answer and to tell to this people that I am not obliged to know the name of all the United States states.

I see the Italian Newspapers of New York will receive Tetrazzini with a scandal. Nice thing for they to do! I think there is somebody who pay to let gat Tetrazzini seek and dont let her sing. You see, dearest, under how many bad propositions are the

225

artists. I am sure that some agent (theatrical) who care for the interest of some other artist pay the press to put down Tetrazzini. This is very bad because that means not let work the people.

Now you immagine in 17 years which I am here how many people try to put me down, with lots lies. Fortunately they dont go further but I suffered greateel.

What devil interest to the public a private life of an artist? This is happen only in this country where the liberty is enchained with heavy chains.

Too bad for the poor fat one! I hope she have the cleverness to not bring with her, her Toto.

The day which I will stop to let talking of me will be the most happy one of my life.

You know dearest, many times I wish to myself some unfortunate thing, to let me go out of this business, because I am tired of it. You will say, "Why you dont stop?" I am thinking of that from long ago but they dont let me. You will see when the contract of the Metropolitan will finish! I am sure that before this contract will be over, Gatti come with some proposition.

It is terrible and I think even after I die people dont let me alone.

We will refuse everyone because we wish to live and enjoy of the life. It is true, dearest? Yes, we will live out of the world and enjoy of our life with our sweet Gloria to whom we will devote all the rest of our life. . . .

I send you with my mind all my lovely thoughts.

Your
Rico

Rice Hotel, Houston, Texas.

Oct 21 1920 3 p.m.

My Doro dearest:

. . . I went to see the hall and is very sordo [deadening]. Bad acustick. There was somebody fixing chairs on the stage and when I ask Coppicus why he said, "There will be chairs all around." All my blod came on my head and I felt very nervous because he know that I dont want people back to me when I sing, and have had a fight for that in Chicago and St. Paul. I jomp on him and I dont know what I said. I left him and went away.

Fucito came here and told me that Coppicus decided to take away all the chaires from the stage. You see, if I dont say anything he will put people even between my legs when I walk.

The newspaper mans just goes away. What a noise, my dear, this people. They want know things I dont know. I am tired of them.

I think I am a little tired of everything, and I need to live a little outside of the world, to let me forget and let people forget me.

I leave you now with my pen but not with my heart.

Your own
Rico

P. S. I am at the 12th floor of this hotel, in two rooms which they call the most beautiful and expences suite; in effect they charge for $50 a day. Here are many things and nothing comfy. Coppicus is angry because he pay the $50 and not I.

In train after been passed Atlanta Ga.

Oct 24 1920 6 p.m.

My Doro mine:

If this train will loose his mind, I means, if the man who control the engine goes crazy and not stop at any stations, letting go the engine until she can, do you think we will arrive in New York? Ah! That will be fine and I will be so glad! But alas! There is two man whom control the engine and there is not enough coal to arrive to New York! I dont know why I have in my mind that the train bring me directly home. Perhaps is the avidity to be there!

. . . Too bad about the old restaurant keeper, Pane. That is the life. Work, work, and after six foot of ground and good bye!

Five days more, sweetheart, and I will be near you and Baby. My! What a joy will be for us! We will have a good time like little children. I love you, sweetheart.

Your

Rico

The Selwyn Charlotte N.C.

Oct 24 1920 10.15 p.m.

My own Doro:

It is half an hour that I arrived here in very tired condition. Two long days and one night in the train. Too much even with confort. At the station here I found a big crowd of people waiting for "Cruso," and there was applause and talking, as "He is fatty!" "He is big man!" "There he is. Now I can go to bed!" "I am glad he is here because I am interested in 75 dollars." I dont know what this one means but seams that there was 75 dollars of tickets bought from one family.

I was so happy in looking the pictures of Gloria and tears came on my eyes as a joy.

I love you. And more time pass more my love for you cames big and big.

I wish you were in myself to see how I love you! What can I do to let you be certenly of that? I think I done all my best to show you my love and I am steel trying do things to let you be convinced of it. Be sure that your Rico adore you and he adored you from the first time he meet you. In my solitude I thought always to this tall girl with blue eyes, and from whom I heard the first sweet voice which come right through my heart!

Five days more! Ah! I am happy!

I embrace you, my heart.

Your
Rico.

In train from Charlotte to Norfolk.
Oct 26 1920 Noon.

My Doro darling:

I forget to tell you about something happen yesterday afternoon. After I have finish write to you, I lait down to a loung for little rest. Suddenly somebody knock at the door. I said, "Came in!" Nobody came. I went at the door. Nobody was there. Mario, who was in his room in front of my door and to whom I ask about, he said that he saw a girl pass quickly. I look in the corridor and nobody was there. I went back to my loung. After a while the same knock. I jomping up, open the door and nothing. Zirato was in Mario's room and I asked to go to see around the corner of the corridor. He start but from the corner came a little girl about ten years old. Zirato ask very rude to this girl if she was the one who knocked at my door. "Are you Cruso?" said the girl. "No," said Zirato, "But you have no right to knock at his door." I was at the door and I saw the girl trembling, and I said, "I am Cruso, what you wish?" She came to me all trembling and took my hand and put up her little face and say, "Oh, Mr Cruso! I just wish to know how is your little Gloria!" And steel trembling she caress my hand and look with her big eyes in mine, waiting for an answer. You dont immagine the effect which this asking produced in me. I caressed her and beg to calm because I thought she will fall down on my feet. I assure her that our dear baby was allright, and when she was calm, she ask about you, about my concert and lots of things. Cute little girl!

In the night at the concert there was a box addressed to Mrs Caruso. I opened it and there was a bung of flowers. The card say from a florist. I dont pay any attention because there was no name, and I give the flowers away. But just few moment go, Miss Miriam, to whom I give the flowers, and told the story of the little girl, told me that she think that this flowers was sending from the girl because nobody also talk about you and nobody have interest to send flowers to me for you that are far away. Poor little girl! So kind of her. Sorry dont know her name to send her our best thanks.

I kiss you both with all my soul. My Doro of gold! I love you!

Rico

230

Chapter Twelve

I HAD never seen Enrico look so weary and worn as on the day
he returned to New York. The tour had been even harder than
he had expected and his cold, instead of disappearing, had
descended to his chest. The fact that he scarcely spoke about his
health made me know that he was really worried, for only when
things were not serious did he complain. Once a chorus man ac-
cidentally trod on his bare foot in *Samson*. He limped through
the rest of the opera, was carried groaning to his car and treated
at home by a doctor waiting with a pharmacy of remedies. After
he was nicely bandaged and tucked in bed he said to me con-
fidingly, "I like to make fussy sometimes." Not even a little
mark could be discovered on his foot.

The opera season was to begin with *La Juive* on the fifteenth
of November, and it was already the last day of October. Besides
the necessity of an intensive restudy of his role, which he hadn't
sung since Havana, there were many important tasks awaiting
him—interviews with reporters about the tour, with insurance
agents about the robbery, with lawyers about new contracts; there
were taxes and bills to be paid and hundreds of letters to be
written.

His cold was keeping him awake at night and at last he decided
to see his doctor. I don't know who recommended this Dr. H.
Enrico had consulted nerve specialists, chiropractors and osteo-
paths as well as ordinary practitioners, but all had failed to dis-
cover the cause of his headaches. For some reason of his own he
believed that Dr. H. would succeed.

I didn't like Dr. H. I had seen him give Enrico ridiculous treatments the year before for his headaches. These treatments consisted in laying him on a metal table, placing zinc plates on his stomach and sandbags on top of them. An electric current was then passed through the plates, and the spasmodic jerking of the bags was supposed to produce a super massage which would break up fat and cure the headaches. Next he was put in an electric cabinet and dehydrated. When it was all over he weighed several pounds less—which he regained, as soon as he got home, by drinking quarts of water. Of course his headaches continued. Since I couldn't prevent him from going to this doctor I didn't speak of my skepticism or protest when, one raw November day, he went again to Dr. H. to receive the same treatment for a cold in the chest that he had been given for a pain in the head.

* * *

The opera season opened with the usual enthusiastic audiences; performance followed performance in rhythmic succession. Our life at home was quiet, happy, busy. Instead of working over his clippings in the evenings, Enrico was now more interested in classifying his ancient gold coins, which were to be added to his famous collection in Signa. Sometimes Gloria played in her pen on the floor beside us as we worked. When she pulled herself up on her little feet and called "Daddy," he would push back his chair, hurry to her, lift her up in his arms and cover her face with kisses.

As Christmas approached, Enrico began to make a long list of names—people to whom he always gave presents. When he read it to me I was appalled. "But, Rico, you don't like all these people?" "No," he said, "but they expect."

To go Christmas shopping with Enrico was a lovely adventure. He bought what he had planned to buy, never asked the price

232

and chose his presents at only two places—his favorite antique shop and Tiffany's. At Tiffany's he bought gold souvenirs for everyone who didn't like antiques, and at the antiquarian's he bought antiques for everyone who didn't like souvenirs.

He walked through the aisles of Tiffany's, looking very large in his fur-lined coat, while his good face with its great warm smile expressed the real spirit of Christmas and the happiness he was feeling. He stopped at a counter and peered into the lighted case. "Look, Doro, nice little boxes for powder and for red." The salesman dropped his professional boredom and became charged with excitement.

"Please, the little boxes," said Enrico, pointing not with one finger but with his whole hand—a gesture that to me symbolized the limitless generosity of his heart. He examined the design of each box with fastidious care and finally chose four.

"We like fifty like this, then thirty like this, ten like this, and one like this." The clerk stammered that he would find out if so many were available. We went on to cigarette cases across the aisle, where the order he gave was equally staggering. Then we examined the bracelets and neck chains. By this time everyone in Tiffany's knew that Caruso was doing his Christmas shopping and the manager came to greet us.

"Very much obliged," said Enrico and shook him warmly by the hand. "I like now to give you special order."

We sat about a table while Enrico made rough sketches of the design he wanted for a gold watch charm—this year's gift to his closest friends. "You will make twenty like this and send."

We shook hands with everyone, left the shop without any idea of how much money we had spent and went on to the antiquarian's. There Enrico chose gifts according to the recipient's taste, not his own. "This is very ugly and I dislike it very much, but they collect and find interesting."

He had one friend, however, for whom he always selected a gift such as he would have bought for his own collection. She was an imperial little old lady—Mrs. Ogden Goelet. They had been friends for many years, and Enrico had a deep and enduring affection for her. She had the first box in the Golden Horseshoe and he never failed to smile up at her as soon as he came out on the stage. On the morning after a new opera he always sent her an autographed score and she always telephoned to thank him for singing so beautifully. Once we invited her to lunch with us in our little Italian restaurant. She had never been to such a place before and she loved it. Enrico enveloped her with almost filial tenderness, as he watched her little hands in their white suède gloves struggling with a big plate of spaghetti.

Our last errand of the day was to call at the bank to fetch bags of gold pieces—gifts for the chorus and employees of the Metropolitan and for the entire staff of the Vanderbilt Hotel.

* * *

One day while we were driving in the park Enrico was seized with a chill. Instead of returning home he insisted on going to his doctor, who gave him another of those fearful treatments. Afterward, with every pore open, he went out into the winter air. No one knows why singers are more susceptible to cold than other people—perhaps their fear sensitizes them. Before night Enrico had a dull pain in his left side and began to cough.

Pagliacci was scheduled for the following week, and I knew he would insist on singing, though day by day his cough was growing worse. I began to live under the intense nervous strain that was soon to become a primary condition of our life. On the day of the performance I noticed an occasional shadow of pain pass across his face, and as he left for the theater he said, "Doro, be on time and pray for me."

234

When he came out on the stage and looked up at me with weary anxious eyes I felt I couldn't bear to stay seated in the crimson velvet box, silent and unprotesting. I hated all the eager enraptured faces, shining like masks in the light from the stage against the blackened house. My heart was stricken with pity for him, but all I could do to help was to sit still and smile.

As he began to sing "*Vesti la giubba*," I watched every movement he made and every expression of his face. He reached the high A in his aria . . . and his voice broke. From the angle of my box I saw him stumble toward the wings. Zirato was waiting there and caught him in his arms as he fell. Instantly the curtain was brought down.

I hurried to the dressing room and was with him when he regained consciousness. "It was only the pain in my side," he explained. "Go back to the box so they will think I am all right." When Dr. H. arrived he strapped Enrico's side and said, "Nothing serious—only a little attack of intercostal neuralgia. He may continue now."

The audience, nervous from the long unexpected wait, watched me as I entered. "He tripped on the step," I said to the occupants of the next box. In a few minutes the house was rustling with the news. Then the lights were lowered and the second act began. He sang it through without showing a sign of pain.

As the lights went up I heard a woman say, "Wonderful performance—I wouldn't have missed it for worlds." But Enrico said, "I hope never again to have such pain—it made me sicky all over and the world black."

* * *

Only three days later he had to appear in his most exhausting role, Nemorino in *L'Elisir d'amore*, at the Brooklyn Academy of Music. Again his doctor told him he was well enough to sing, but I was filled with apprehension.

235

CARUSO AS NEMORINO IN *L'Elisir d'Amore*

Before the performance I went as usual to his dressing room and found him standing at the washstand, rinsing his throat. Suddenly I heard him say, "Look!" I looked and saw that the water in the basin was pink. "Darling, you brushed your teeth too hard," I said. He took another mouthful and spat it out. This time the water was red. Mario said quietly, "I have the doctor's number." I said, "Tell him to bring adrenalin."

Enrico continued silently to wash his throat. Each time he said, "Look." At last he stopped. "Doro," he said, "return to your place and no matter what happens do not move. The audience will be watching you, so be careful not to start a panic."

I obeyed, sick with fear, remembering that he had once said, "Tenors die sometimes on the stage after big note, from hemorrhage."

My seats were in the front row. The curtain rose a quarter of an hour late, and I knew that the doctor must have arrived. The four long acts of gaiety began, on a stage filled with moving color and bright melody. Enrico came running out over the little rustic bridge, laughing and looking as foolish and stupid as possible. He wore a red wig, a pongee smock, brown breeches and striped stockings; a big red cotton handkerchief hung out of his pocket and he carried a little basket over his arm. The audience applauded wildly. Standing close to the footlights, he began at once to sing. When he had finished he turned his back and reached for his handkerchief. I heard him give a little cough, but he came in on his cue, finished the phrase and turned away again. When he faced the audience I saw that the front of his smock was scarlet. A whisper blew through the house but stopped as he began to sing. This time it was an aria and he couldn't turn his back. From the wings Zirato's hand held out a towel. Enrico took it, wiped his lips and went on singing. Towel after towel was passed to him and still he sang on. All about him on the stage lay crimson towels. At last he finished the aria and ran off. The act was ended and the curtain came down.

Cold and blind with terror, I sat without moving. For long moments the theater was as silent as an empty house. Then, as if a signal had been given, a thunder of sound and movement shook the audience. I heard shouts and screams, voices crying "Stop him!" "Don't let him go on!"

Someone touched my shoulder. "I am Judge Dyke, Mrs. Caruso. May I escort you to the dressing room?" I rose and took his arm. We walked slowly up the aisle but when I reached the corridor I began to run.

Surrounded by terrified faces, Enrico was lying on a couch. Dr. H. was explaining that a little vein had burst at the base of the tongue, and Mr. Ziegler, assistant manager of the Metropolitan, was pleading with Enrico to go home. For the first time in his life he didn't protest but consented that the audience be dismissed.

On the way home in the car he didn't speak of the catastrophe but sat with his eyes closed, holding my hand. "I am very tired, Doro," he said, but by the time we reached the hotel I saw that he had been able to restore himself. With his customary authority he insisted on Zirato and the doctor coming upstairs with us, refused to go to bed, ordered supper and sat with us while we ate. It might have been any evening after a performance, except that it was early and he wasn't smoking. An hour later he went to bed and fell asleep immediately.

I lay awake in the darkness and listened to his restless turning. At three o'clock he said, "I must have air." He left his bed and hurried to the open window. For a moment he stared down at the street below, then began to climb over the sill. I do not know how I reached him in time. I put my arms around him and dragged him back. Without a word he lay down on his bed and

238

slept again. Perhaps he had had a dream. We did not speak of it, and I think he never remembered.

The next day he was better and refused to stay in bed. Preparations for Christmas continued—a phantom Christmas, since Enrico could not hide his suffering. Still the doctor insisted that it was nothing but "intercostal neuralgia," and to relieve the pain he merely added more tapes and strapped them tighter and tighter. Enrico sang, on the thirteenth and sixteenth, encased in a corset of adhesive as unyielding as a coat of mail. On the twenty-first he was to sing *Elisir*, but that morning his pain was so acute that I myself sent for Dr. H. He laughed at our anxiety, changed the tapes and bleated again, "Intercostal neuralgia." Gatti came and went during the day, and by four o'clock we all knew that Enrico could not sing that night. By resting for three days he would be well enough for his Christmas Eve performance of *La Juive*.

Gloria's first Christmas tree was set up in the salon—a tall and perfect tree, glittering with snow and bells and tinseled stars. She sat in her high chair, staring at it, and when her father came in she shrieked with delight and pointed at the colored toys. "You like, then?" he said, sitting down in a chair beside her. "I too." Together they watched Mario hang the last bright ball. They always enchanted each other and this mutual spell increased their resemblance. It was so striking that I spoke of it.

"But she has not this," Enrico said, touching the cleft in his chin. "They say it shows strong character, but I tell you a secret. With me it is not so—it is a sign of weak head. When I was a little boy in Naples I took a big piece of bread that was my supper, to eat it sitting on the doorstep. The bread was very hard so I say, 'Why not put a little water on to make nice and soft?' So I walk to a fountain that I like very much. This fountain was not near so I think I take a streetcar, but I have no money. Then what I do? I run after streetcar and jump on its back and quick it goes and I fall off on my chin. I make a big cut and lose my bread and go home crying. This scar then shows the weak head because I, and not God, made it."

Although for twenty-four hours Enrico had felt nothing more than a dull ache in his side, I didn't want him to sing on Christmas Eve. Gatti, too, was anxious and came to see us while Dr. H. was there. "Do you think he should sing?" Gatti asked him. "There is nothing the matter with his voice," was the reply.

I stayed at home on Christmas Eve to prepare a surprise for Enrico, and this was the only performance of his in New York I ever missed except when Gloria was born. When he left for the theater Enrichetta, Brunetta and I set to work to arrange a beautiful crèche in the salon. Electric lights had already been installed in the chimney to shine down on the manger in the fireplace, and about the hearth stood shepherds and kings with their gifts. I had invited Enrico's friends to come in after the opera for a supper such as is always given in Naples on Christmas Eve—eels prepared in five different ways, hot and cold octopus and all kinds of little fishes fried in oil and dried. I didn't find any of these dishes very good.

When Enrico returned I met him at the door. Although his eyes were eager, his face was the color of clay, as if the blood beneath had turned gray. He was touched by the crèche, amused by the supper and glad to see his friends, but he didn't join in their laughter with his usual exuberance. "I think better I take only a cup of consommé," he said. Dr. H. was there too—the only time he was welcome, as far as I was concerned, because he took a fishbone out of my throat.

240

After everyone had gone I asked Enrico about the performance. "They liked," he said, "but my side hurt—not strong but much."

That performance of *La Juive* was the last he ever sang, and I was not there to hear him.

* * *

Christmas Day was beautiful. The apartment was filled with cold sunshine and the smell of the fir tree. From eight in the morning the doorbell rang continuously as messengers brought gifts, flowers and telegrams. Enrico came to join Gloria and me in the salon and laid a big box in my arms. "Hope you will like this —it take two years to find, in South America." In the box was a magnificent chinchilla coat that had cost thousands and thousands of dollars—and much as I loved it I couldn't tell him that the only gift I wanted was for him to be well and strong again. Gloria's special present was a string of amber beads longer than she was—"In Italy we say that amber keep sore throat away."

A pile of little coin boxes lay open on the table, and Enrico went to the safe to fetch the bags of gold. He poured a handful of the shining coins on the tray of Gloria's high chair. "Here, Puschina, play with these. Now I dress quickly, Doro, and we take our presents to the people at the theater. Can you make nice in the little boxes?" I said they would be ready as soon as he was, and he left us.

Baby played with the gold pieces and I began to fill the boxes . . . a hundred dollars for Philip, the old property man . . . fifty for the wigmaker . . . I had gone down the long list as far as "Five for each of the chorus" when I heard Enrico scream. As I rushed from the room he screamed again. I reached his dressing room at the same time as Zirato and Mario. Scream after scream came from the bathroom. Mario flung open the door and with

241

superhuman strength lifted Enrico from the tub. His shrieks rang through the apartment as Zirato and Mario carried him, wrapped in his white robe, to the couch. He sat there on the edge, leaning forward, while streams of sweat ran down his face and dripped to the floor.

I ran to the telephone and within three minutes Dr. Murray, the hotel doctor, arrived. He didn't wait to examine Enrico but gave him an injection of codeine and, a few minutes later, a second one. Gradually the screams stopped. "He'll sleep for an hour now," said the doctor. "You'd better call his own physician. I'll be in my office after lunch if you need me."

Ten minutes later Enrico opened his eyes—and shrieked. Zirato, who had been unable to find Dr. H., began frantically telephoning one doctor after another. At last I could bear the screams no longer. I found the bottle of ether in his bathroom, soaked a handkerchief and held it against his face. Slowly he lost consciousness, but his moans were so frightening that I put my fingers in my ears.

I don't know how long I stood there, but at last the door opened and I saw a tall man dressed in tweeds, with an American face. "I'm Dr. Evan Evans," he said. His examination of Enrico was swift and expert and his diagnosis instantaneous. "Mrs. Caruso, your husband has acute pleurisy, probably going into pneumonia." He turned to Mario and Zirato. "Sit him up in that chair, carry him to his room and put him to bed, with lots of pillows. Then call me. And now let me see that baby, Gloria."

I shall never forget the relief I felt, and the gratitude, for the strength and assurance of that man. An hour later a trained nurse was in charge and there was little left for me to do. I gathered up the scattered gold pieces, sent them to the theater and arranged the forgotten flowers.

The doctor had paid his last visit, the frightened servants had gone to bed. I said good night to Nanny, kissed the baby's unconscious face, went back into the salon and sat down. Around the tree and on the tables lay the unopened presents. Enrico was sleeping peacefully. Christmas was over and the house was quiet.

Chapter Thirteen

THE NEXT morning Dr. Evans called into consultation Drs. Samuel Lambert, Antonio Stella and Francis Murray of the hotel. They were all in complete agreement—the acute pleurisy had developed into bronchial pneumonia.

I didn't realize the serious complications that sometimes follow pleurisy. Three days later as the nurse and I were standing at the foot of Enrico's bed, his face suddenly turned the color of slate and he began to gasp. "Quick, an oxygen tank!" cried the nurse. As if by a miracle Dr. Stella opened the door at that moment. He snatched an aspirating needle from his bag and plunged it into Enrico's back. As the fluid in the pleural cavity was drawn off, lessening the pressure on his heart, his face lost its dreadful color and he began to breathe freely. . . . I realized I had seen death approach a human being, and turn away.

The doctors decided that a major operation was imperative in order to guard against another such crisis. We called in the great surgeon, Dr. John Erdman, and overnight our beautiful salon was transformed into an operating room. Enrico wanted to know exactly what was going to be done to him, and I explained that an incision would be made in his back to remove the fluid that remained in the pleural cavity.

I wasn't present during the operation, but Dr. Erdman told me later that when he made the incision a dark liquid burst out with such force that it hit the opposite wall. A gallon of this fluid was drawn off and a drain inserted between the ribs. Dr. Stella said it was fortunate that the ribs were far enough apart to permit this draining tube to pass between them, since otherwise it would have been necessary to remove a piece of bone and Enrico might never have sung again.

The operation was successful. In two days his temperature was normal and, although the sound of his breath whistling through the tube disturbed him, the wound drained well and caused him no pain. Dr. Stella congratulated him on the spacing of his ribs, and Enrico asked in alarm, "You mean if my rib was cut I never sing again?" The doctor laughed. "Your rib was not cut, so don't worry about it. You are going to sing better than ever."

* * *

Since the beginning of Enrico's illness I had been troubled by a problem that was both embarrassing and delicate. The problem was Dr. H. He regarded himself as physician in chief and treated Enrico and me accordingly. He ran in at all hours, awakened his patient and often remained late into the night. He told Enrico that he disagreed with the other doctors, insisted that he knew the case better than they did and that his diagnosis was still "intercostal neuralgia with a possible complication of intestinal toxemia." Each visit left poor Enrico bewildered and nervous; and when I discovered that he had been given an unprescribed treatment at three o'clock in the morning, unknown to the other doctors, I decided that it was time to act.

The next day I waited for Dr. H. in the studio, from where I could watch the front door. When I saw him tripping toward me down the corridor, I think I have never felt such anger. I said, "Dr. H., I do not want you to come here again. Please leave now and never come back." My voice was shaking. He didn't answer me, but started toward Enrico's door. I blocked his way. "If you take one more step I'll drop you out of that window." He fled down the corridor, and I never saw him again.

* * *

In the weeks that followed, Enrico was a patient and polite invalid, obeying every instruction the doctors gave him. But he didn't like trained nurses; he couldn't understand why women should wait on him, and he was annoyed by their rigid insistence on their duties. One day his old authority returned. "Doro," he said, "tell nicely to the *signorina* I wish that she stays in the salon. Mario will remain here with me and if we need her we will send for." I bought him a little gold bell, engraved with his name, to ring when he needed her. It had a sweet sound, but I didn't hear it often.

Every day I had lunch by his bedside. He would eat only the food that Mario cooked for him—dishes of his childhood, such as lentil soup and semolina. In the afternoon he amused himself by modeling in clay and making caricatures of the doctors and nurses. Gatti, anxious and nervous, was one of the few visitors he was permitted to see. Mr. Child also came, and congratulated Enrico for having already made twenty-eight of the required forty records which his ten-year contract called for.

I thought he was nearly well, but one morning in early February he woke with a high temperature. By night it had risen to 104. The doctors assembled again and I waited in the salon until Dr. Lambert joined me after the consultation. As we sat side by side on the sofa, facing the Madonna, he patted my hand and said, "The drainage is imperfect—Dr. Erdman must operate again to-morrow." But when he added, "Don't worry, we still have a lot of rope left," I knew that it had suddenly become a matter of life and death.

We thought it best not to tell Enrico of the operation until the next morning, thus sparing him a night of apprehension. When the operating table was set up and the doctors and the

246

anesthetist had arrived, I went to Enrico. He listened to me without a word, then asked for Dr. Erdman. "Doctor," he said, "I do not like not to know when something must happen to me. Send everybody away and say that I will have the operation not today but tomorrow."

The next morning, February 12, Dr. Erdman reopened the incision. The poison he found in the deepest part of the cavity had become so viscid that now only the most drastic drainage could save his life. For this it was necessary to remove four inches of rib. . . . As soon as the operation was over I begged the doctors never to let Enrico know what had been done to him.

Dr. Murray waited with me for him to come out of the anesthetic. Hours passed, but he still remained unconscious. At eight that evening the doctors returned and pronounced that his deep sleep was in reality a state of coma. Dr. Stella said, "Mrs. Caruso, you must try to rouse him by any means you can think of." I called his name and kissed him again and again. Mario, weeping, begged him to speak and Zirato implored him to come back to us. But Enrico looked at nothing through half-closed lids and said, "Ba-ba-ba" over and over again. Dr. Murray moved into the apartment that night, and two more nurses were engaged.

Each day I carried Gloria to his bedside, and even sent for Mimmi to come home from Culver, hoping in vain that the sound of his children's voices might reach through his coma.

The newspapers telephoned continuously and finally the editors asked me to permit reporters to remain in the apartment. They established themselves in the dining room to receive the doctors' bulletins, and these were published in every new edition. The hotel manager told me that hundreds of people called every day to inquire about Caruso and went away weeping. Early each morning six Italian laborers came to the hotel to ask how Caruso had slept before starting their work on the big pipes under Thirty-fourth Street.

Thus ten days passed. For me there was no longer any movement of time, or any separation of night from day. The doctors had done everything they could and now there was no more "rope." I looked into a face I did not recognize, drained of all expression, shrunken and empty. He never stirred, he scarcely seemed to breathe. Only the faint movement of his lips as he repeated "Ba-ba-ba" assured me that he was still alive.

At noon on the tenth day, as Dr. Stella was watching with me as usual beside the bed, Zirato announced that the Italian Ambassador was calling to pay his respects. The doctor left the room and returned a moment later with the Ambassador, Rolando Ricci. He was a tall thin man with a gray beard and he wore a pink carnation in his buttonhole. He kissed my hand without speaking, and stood looking down at Enrico for a long moment. Then, bending close to his face, he said in a slow firm voice, "Caruso! I come with a message to you from your country and your king. They want you to live." Minutes seemed to pass. Then I heard a faint voice speaking. "Let me die in my country."

"The last time I heard you sing was in Lisbon—*Carmen*," said the Ambassador. He took the pink carnation from his coat and laid it in Enrico's hand.

"Not *Carmen*—it was *Le Cid*," whispered Enrico. He tried to raise the flower to his lips, but it was too heavy. He gave a long sigh and fell into a natural sleep.

* * *

During Enrico's illness thousands of letters had arrived from every part of the world. Children wrote that they were praying for him; priests and rabbis asked their congregations to join in

248

special supplications; simple old Italians wrote of old remedies—massage with onions, or wilted lettuce leaves hung around the neck; others sent blessed rosaries and medals, holy pictures and even relics of saints. These I hung on the walls around the Madonna, and as soon as Enrico was out of danger I wrote my thanks to each giver.

One day as I sat in the studio, answering letters, the door at the end of the hall opened and a man came in. He walked rapidly down the long corridor, straight to my desk, placed his hands upon it and shouted, "I am Jesus Christ and I have come to see Caruso." "You must speak to his secretary," I replied and hastily called Zirato.

This incident made us realize that our door must be watched, and I knew the man who would guard it with his life—old Schol, chief of the Metropolitan claque by night, umbrellamaker by day. The adoration of this little German Jew for Enrico was beyond anything I have ever known. After every performance at the Metropolitan he was always waiting at the stage entrance to open the door of Enrico's car and hear the beloved voice say, "Ah, Schol. Good night and thank you." Even when Enrico sang outside of New York, Schol always came to perform this happy service. Once he had been greatly rewarded. It was just before Enrico was to record "Eli Eli" in Hebrew for the Victor Company. We were returning from an out-of-town concert and, knowing that Schol was on the train, Enrico sent Zirato to bring him to our compartment.

Schol sat on the edge of the seat, waiting for Enrico to speak. With his long smooth flat face and his cap of white hair he looked like an illustration of an old nursery rhyme.

"Schol, can you tell me how to say these words?"

The little man took the sheet of music that Enrico held out to him and read it through. "Yes, I can tell you, Signor Caruso."

He meticulously taught Enrico how to pronounce each word, then rose, bowed and left us. Touched by the look of dignity and pride on the old man's face, Enrico said, "Schol is my really friend, and I am his. We have not many, him and me."

And so it was Schol who was chosen to sit at a little table in the corridor outside the entrance to our apartment, with a book spread out before him for visitors to sign. He was no longer Schol the umbrellamaker, but Michael the archangel, guarding the gate of heaven.

Chapter Fourteen

WHEN Enrico was strong enough to get up for a short time each day, X rays were taken of his chest. They revealed that his left lung had contracted. Naturally we concealed this fact from him and arranged that he should not see the plates.

In the early part of his convalescence he complained of his right hand. "What happens to my fingers?" he asked the doctors, "they feel like the foot when asleep." Although the doctors couldn't account for this tingling sensation, it grew worse as time went on and the flesh began visibly to shrink away from the bones. I often saw him staring at his hand in bewilderment.

He received only a few visitors and tired easily. Once I took him in a wheel chair to our garden on the roof, but he didn't enjoy it. "I wait to walk by myself," he said unhappily. After that day he walked a little around the apartment, leaning on my arm as he studied the offerings that covered the wall. "So many people pray for me—that is strange," he said.

He often spoke longingly of going to Italy for the summer. From a seed catalogue he planned a garden for Signa and cabled to Martino the names of all the flowers he wanted him to plant. It did him good to talk of his country, of the bright fields and the warm slow movement of peasant life. I remembered walking with him one morning on a road above the Bay of Naples and seeing a boy, ragged, dirty and beautiful, lying on a low wall. When he saw us he sat up and held out his hand, asking for a penny. Enrico said, "And if I don't give you a penny, what then?" "Then, *signor*, I will still have the sun." That boy was the Italy Enrico longed for.

And then, one afternoon, while I was playing with Gloria, the nurse came to the door, holding a thermometer.

"How much?" I asked.

"A hundred and one and a half."

I sent for the doctors.

Dr. Erdman's examination disclosed that a deep abscess had developed between the hip and the ribs, due to the poisonous seepage from the pleura. He would have to operate again, and this time without a general anesthetic because of Enrico's weakened heart. I felt a sick horror. "Won't that hurt him too much, Doctor?" He answered, "I don't know. I will do my best."

When I told Enrico, his hopeless eyes looked up at me and filled with tears as he pleaded with me not to let them hurt him again. While the doctors prepared the instruments I knelt beside him, looking into his anguished face. Two nurses held his feet down, I held his hands and Zirato held a towel between his teeth. Dr. Erdman injected cocaine, waited for it to take effect, then picked up the scalpel . . . Enrico's screams were fearful. In a few minutes the abscess was located. I watched Dr. Erdman break it and pack the wound with gauze.

In twenty-four hours his temperature was normal and in two days he was well. But in a week another abscess formed, followed by another operation; and within ten days the whole ghastly procedure had to be gone through again. Nothing is worse than to see someone you love suffer, yet it was the very strength of my love which gave me the courage to be present during the operations. The fourth abscess couldn't be located and his suffering during the probing was beyond human endurance. His screams came forth on a continuous note with all the power of his famous voice, and that voice was beautiful even when it screamed. After the surgeon had decided that he could do nothing more until the following day and had dressed the wound, Enrico looked up at him from tortured eyes and said, "Thank you. So sorry." Tears ran down the doctor's cheeks as he pressed the wasted hand.

During the night Enrico's temperature kept climbing and it was obvious that he was growing weaker. At two o'clock in the morning I was sitting in the studio, trying to put together a jigsaw puzzle to keep my mind off a number on a thermometer. Dr. Stella appeared in the doorway and beckoned. "Come, Madame Caruso," he said, "it is his heart—he may have only ten minutes to live." I walked with him past the Madonna and all the little holy pictures around her. As we reached the door he said, "Don't frighten him."

I sat down on a chair beside the bed and listened. He was breathing. The nurses were injecting ether and oil of camphor into his arms. I looked at the still figure outlined under the sheet, and at the thin unconscious face, and I felt that by remaining as motionless as he I could pour into him all my strength and youth and health—that I alone now could keep him alive. . . . I sat like this, without moving even the end of a finger, for seven hours. Once I heard a nurse say, "The pulse is stronger." Later I heard Dr. Stella say, "I think he'll live. . . ."

Dr. Murray touched my arm. "It's all right now, Mrs. Caruso. Go and rest—it's nine o'clock." I walked to the door and fainted.

When I opened my eyes I was lying on a couch in the nursery and Nanny was giving Gloria her breakfast. "She has eaten her first egg," she said. Ah, the beautiful normal life of the nursery!

That morning the doctor located the abscess at once. Although it drained perfectly, Enrico's weakness continued and after several days it was decided to give him a blood transfusion.

The donor was Everett Wilkinson of Meriden, Connecticut, and he said afterward, "I wouldn't change places today with the king of England!" But Enrico said, "I have no more my pure Italian blood—what now am I?"

From that day he began to recover and the doctors told him that he could go to Italy in a few weeks if he took great care of himself during his convalescence. I think this promise made him well.

We planned that he should take a long rest, even for a year; stay two months in Sorrento, where he could take mud baths to cure his hand, and then in the autumn go to Signa in time for the grape gathering. The peasants always made a fete of their first day in the vineyards. The women wore bright-colored head-cloths and coarse linen blouses that had been washed in the running water of the village fountain and slapped on the smooth stones until they were as white as milk; their full black cotton skirts fell a little below their knees and their legs and feet were bare. The men wore big straw hats trimmed with long ribbons. When everything was ready we would go down to the vineyard, greet the workers with wishes for a rich harvest and ceremoniously pick the first bunch of grapes. All morning they laughed and sang as they tossed the purple clusters into barrels that stood on low carts drawn by white oxen. Later they would press out the first wine with their feet, as they had for centuries; they refused to use the modern winepress Enrico had installed, just as they refused, even while admiring, the big threshing machine he had sent from America, preferring to beat the grain on stone floors with their flails. At midday we sent bread, goat cheese and flasks of cool wine to the vineyards, and after the peasants had eaten and drunk they lay down in the shade of the vines to sleep while the oxen stood motionless, their bodies steaming and their feet buried deep in the warm red earth. At twilight the creaking carts

254

moved slowly up the steep road to the villa farm, the singing peasants walking beside them, their voices drowned by the droning of clouds of bees that swarmed over the barrels of sweet bruised grapes.

Early in May Enrico ordered Mario and Punzo to begin packing, and told Fucito to prepare the music trunk. He would often sit at the piano, looking through the hundreds of songs that had been sent him during his illness, whistling softly as he turned the pages.

When I went to fetch him for his first drive I found him trying to write in his checkbook, holding the pen with difficulty between his index finger and thumb. On the desk I saw a pair of bright yellow gloves.

"It is only this that does not get well," he said, looking at his trembling hand. "I will wear a glove always. No one will know the really reason—they will say, 'Caruso is a funny man, he wears the glove in the house.' This is my idea—you think good?"

He didn't realize that not only his hand but his whole body had changed. One shoulder drooped, and because he couldn't stand upright he seemed inches shorter. His face had become smaller and older; all his gestures were slow and limited, as if he were still afraid of pain.

"I pay the doctors," he said, as Mario helped him into his coat. "But I not find the bill for my doctor—the one who came no more." "I should think not," I answered, "considering how awful he was." "But I feel to give something, Doro. He did try to be kind. We will drive to the jeweler and I will find a present for his wife for fifteen thousand dollars—that is the smallest bill from any of the other doctors."

The news had spread that Caruso was going out for the first time, and a crowd was waiting to cheer him when we stepped out

255

of the elevator. He walked slowly, smiling and holding my arm. A policeman was trying to control another crowd outside in the street. "Nice people," Enrico said, "they have not forgot me." He had no realization of how anxious the whole world had been, for he hadn't yet been allowed to see all the letters and telegrams that had come during the last five months.

"First we go to the theater," he said. All along our route to the Metropolitan people recognized him and waved.

He looked like the old Caruso as he stood in the executive offices of the opera house, receiving the congratulations of the staff and employees. His back straightened and his voice was firm as he assumed his former air of leadership. The king of the opera had returned to his people.

At the jeweler's he asked to be shown gold-mesh bags. While he was examining them I looked in the other cases and saw a little platinum chain that was perfect for the watch he had brought me from Havana. When I rejoined him he had chosen a bag set with big diamonds and sapphires. "You like this?" he asked. "You think it will please?" I said I thought it was beautiful and that Mrs. H. would be delighted. Then I said, "Enrico, I just saw a little chain for my watch. May I have it? It costs a hundred dollars." He looked at me a moment before answering, "Doro, darling, you know that I have not sung all winter. I have many expenses—I just pay the doctors——" "Oh, Rico, I don't really need the chain at all—a black ribbon would be much better. Please don't think I want it." I felt overcome with shame for having been so thoughtless when he had such enormous bills to pay. I hated myself as I went to wait for him in the car.

When he came out he said, "Let us drive for half-hour." In the park he took a box from his pocket. "I have a present for you," he said and put it in my hand. "Oh! the little platinum chain!" I unwrapped the box and drew out a string of diamonds more than a yard long. "I give you this because it is the first time you ask me for something." Then he gave me a second box, saying, "And I give you this because you ask with such sweetness." It was a ring, with one perfect black pearl. I took the hand in the yellow glove and held it against my cheek.

* * *

We were all to sail on the *President Wilson*—Gloria and Nanny, Brunetta and Mario, Enrichetta and Punzo; Mimmi would remain behind because he wanted to go to a summer camp.

Thirty-eight trunks were already locked and labeled; only the music trunk remained open. We were taking Gloria's crib, pen, collapsible gocarts for deck and street, her personal icebox, her bed linen and special pillows, her high chair, her phonograph, her private library, her fabulous toys (though her real devotion was given only to a large pebble and a damp washcloth with which she polished it for hours on end); there were also boxes of zwieback, cartons of cereal and dozens of bottles of Walker-Gordon milk.

While I was telephoning the order for the milk Enrico came in. "When I was a baby I had not special milk," he said. "What did you have—did your mother nurse you?" "No, my mother had no more milk—she had twenty-one children. Twenty boys and one girl—too many. I am number nineteen boy. A lady who was a countess was kind to my mother. Her baby died and she was sad and not come to see my mother so often. So my mother went to her and said, 'I have no milk for little Enrico. Will you give him?' And so she gave me. I think that is the reason for me to be different from my family."

The day before sailing we went out for our last drive. Enrico said we would stop at one place to pay a bill—"I not want to leave owing someone, so we go there first."

I didn't know we were going to the office of the doctor who had taken the X rays. He was out, but his young assistant, whom we had never seen before, received us.

We had already said good-by and were at the door when the young man stopped us. "By the way, Mr. Caruso, your rib has already grown half an inch." My heart turned over.

"My rib?"

There was no way to stop what followed. The young doctor brought Enrico the X-ray plates and showed him where four inches of his rib had been removed.

The door closed behind us. Enrico stood motionless in the corridor and stared at me. "Doro! My rib is gone!"

I took his arm and we walked to the car.

"Do you mind if we go home?" he said. "I do not feel to drive today."

On the way home I waited for him to speak, but he simply said nothing at all. Nor could I find anything to say—he was beyond consolation.

When we reached the apartment he went directly to the studio, where Fucito was packing the scores. "Do not work any more, Fucito," he said, "I have decided not to take with me my music."

I watched him from the door. He walked slowly to the piano and with a gentle gesture closed the lid.

Chapter Fifteen

WE APPROACHED Naples at sunset and saw Vesuvius smoking in the distance. As Enrico and I were standing far out on the ship's bow, Punzo joined us. He had been unusually stupid during the entire trip, unable to remember anything he was told. Now as he stood beside us, gazing at his old city lying in the golden light, Enrico burst out at him. "You are enjoying to be lazy as usual? Have you no head? Do you forget you have work to do? Go then and pack."

After he had gone Enrico said, "Poor Punzo. I tell you something, Doro, only he does not know. I bought for him a nice house in Naples and put money in the bank for him and his wife. He will have big surprise. We will tell no one in Naples that he was my servant—we say he is my assistant. Punzo is a proud man, and here is his home."

After a few days of rest in Naples we sailed across the bay to Sorrento, where we took a floor in the Hotel Vittoria. It was perfect for Enrico, as all the rooms opened on a long covered terrace above the Mediterranean, with Posilipo and Naples in the distance. Our bedroom had deep red tiles and dark blue walls; adjoining it was a smaller room where Enrico could rest after lunch and look at the Italian sky he had so longed to see. The salon was somewhat formal, with Louis XVI furniture and a great gilt piano. I began by disliking this room, but when Enrico told me why it pleased him I liked it too—"All these chairs so stiff and hard will permit people who come to see us to remain not long."

Our meals were served on the terrace and it was there he taught little Gloria her first steps and her first Italian words. All the week he slept and rested, and then one morning he felt strong enough to walk in the hotel gardens and visit the town. We walked very slowly across the sunlit *piazza*. He hadn't walked so far since his illness, and I found many pretexts to stop and rest along the way. Dr. Stella had warned me that he must put no strain on his weak heart, that he must never overtire himself. Above all he advised me to conceal this fact from him, since to worry about it might only retard his progress. Neither did I dare confide this secret to his relatives or friends, knowing that they would immediately repeat it to him. He knew only that there was still one spot in the center of the last incision which hadn't yet healed. It was no bigger than the head of a pin, and each morning I touched it with iodine and covered it with gauze.

On the other side of the *piazza* we stopped before Sorrento's fine old linen shop. Enrico loved and collected beautiful linen, and although the great linen room at Signa already looked like the Grande Maison de Blanc, we went into the shop and ordered dozens of fine sheets, towels with long fringes and exquisite lace tablecloths made by the nuns. "I beginning to put aside for the marriage day of Gloria," he explained.

The population treated him with the loving reverence they might have shown to a great cardinal who had come home after a voyage. He was welcomed with smiles and little words of greeting; children shyly offered him wild flowers and refused his pennies. No one stared, or asked him questions, or tried to shake his hand.

Every day a tub of hot mud arrived from Agnano on the early-morning boat. Mario brought it to the terrace, and while Enrico

260

drank his coffee he held his right hand and arm in the healing clay. He was convinced that in time it would cure him.

Far below our terrace was a little beach where the fishermen left their boats at night. It was there we went to bathe every day in the clear shallow water, and sometimes the fishermen took us out with them in a wide circle to drop the nets. The long scar across Enrico's back became more livid as his skin grew browner. I often saw the men look at it, but they turned their eyes away and asked nothing.

The only people we knew in the hotel were the Italian Ambassador to France, Baron Romano Avezzana, and his American wife, Jacqueline. They called on us one afternoon and Enrico invited them to lunch the following day. The next morning we were standing on our terrace to watch the passengers come off the boat from Naples. There were only two—one tall and thin, with white hair clipped close to his scalp, a brown furrowed face, and pointed white shoes; the other was short and also thin, with flowing hair and a very loud voice; the sleeves of his linen coat hung over his hands and his trousers were pulled up to his armpits by bright red braces; even then they were so long that the rolled-up cuffs looked like rubber rings around his feet. Obviously these men were Neapolitans, for they gesticulated with their whole bodies. I was about to say "Look at those scarecrows" when Enrico gave a shout, "UEI! Arachite! I come down." It was his old sergeant who had first taken him to Maestro Vergine for singing lessons.

When I went downstairs Enrico announced that they were lunching with us. "But you've already invited the Ambassador and his wife." "Yes, that is so," he said, "it will be nice for them to meet my old friends—we will all be friends together."

I thought he had made a mistake, for once, but I was wrong. The pride with which he presented his old friends to his new

261

ones broke down the barriers of birth and position. He made them feel that each was worthy to be the friend of the other, and that he himself was honored to call them all his friends. Throughout the luncheon he poured over them the flow of his rich humanity. When the Neapolitans had left he said, "The little one still wears my suit I gave him, and always without cutting. I tell him he looks funny but he will never cut."

* * *

The weeks drifted by—lovely days of quiet pleasures, hot sunshine and long sweet moonlit nights. Then in July a group of Enrico's New York friends arrived, announcing that they were going to stay several weeks in order to be near him. He was sorry they had come to disturb our peace, but at the same time glad to see familiar faces. Little by little they broke down our restful routine, persuaded him to go on excursions with them or to give dinners on the hotel terrace when the peasants came to dance the tarantella and sing the old Neapolitan songs. I didn't quite know what to do, since I dared not tell them about his heart. Sometimes I would say that I was too tired to go and he also would refuse; but afterward they would describe the fun he had missed and accuse me of wanting to keep him to myself. Finally even Enrico reproached me. "Why you want to spoil my good time, Doro? You must not become lazy and not want to go see beautiful things. I tell my friends tomorrow we lunch with them at Capri."

During the luncheon he talked and laughed with them and then all at once became silent. "I am tired now," he said. "Let us go home." The others tried to stop him, but he turned away impatiently, without saying good-by or thanking them. As soon as we reached the hotel I put him to bed. "You were right, my Doro," he said, "I am not yet fully strong."

For two days he stayed in the apartment, but when he went downstairs again they were waiting for him with new plans. As they knew that he intended to make an offering of thanks for his recovery to the Church of the Madonna of Pompeii, they proposed to go with us and afterward take us to lunch and to visit the ruins. It was then that I realized I must tell them of Dr. Stella's warning. I took them aside and explained how serious might be the consequences of such an outing, but it did no good —they only laughed at my fears and insisted that he should no longer be treated as an invalid. "He's well again, he told us himself he has gained twenty-five pounds."

The road from Sorrento to Pompeii twisted between walls too high to see over and too low to give shade. Beyond them were the dark cool tops of orange trees, but the masses of climbing roses that covered the walls were powdered with white dust. Only the sky gave color, and from time to time there was a flash of blue sea through an open gate.

Sitting in front of us in the car, the two fat men of our party steamed in the heat. They had put handkerchiefs over their heads and their straw hats on top. When we reached the church Enrico told them to wait on the steps for the other car while he and I went inside.

We walked up the long aisle toward the altar. A priest rose from his knees to greet Enrico and they went together into the sacristy. When he rejoined me he was smiling cheerfully. "Ecco— I thanked my Madonna."

The restaurant was as hot as the street and white with light. Through the open windows came the smell of sprinkled dust and sweating donkeys, and the room hummed with the sound of flies. Eight of us sat around a large table set with platters of salami,

263

pickled fish and flasks of heavy red wine. A boy stood behind Enrico's chair and waved a long stick with paper streamers to brush the flies from his plate.

Enrico watched his guests fill their plates with *antipasti*. "I do not eat such things," he said to the fat men. "Madame and I will have chicken and salad." While the others began on their mountains of spaghetti Enrico drank a glass of water and asked the boy to stop waving his stick. When the chicken was brought in he lifted a piece on his fork and examined it. "It smells," he said. But the others went on eating and drinking, talking in loud voices and using Enrico's name as often as possible for the benefit of the waiters. By now their faces were red and glistening and they wiped them with their napkins. Enrico ate a peach, then dipped his hand in a fingerbowl. "It feels fresh," he said, as he moved his poor hand in the cool water.

As usual the news of our plans had run ahead of us and when we arrived at the entrance to the ruins a group of officials was waiting to welcome us. After the handshaking, congratulations and long speeches, the committee told us that by a coincidence Hirohito, the Crown Prince of Japan, had also chosen this day to visit Pompeii and had asked that Caruso be presented. Again a demand on his strength, and again I was powerless to protect him. To make things worse, he refused to be carried in one of the sedan chairs provided for tourists, but started off on foot over the difficult stone road. We came upon Hirohito and his party at the new excavation pit. The future Emperor of Japan had a skinny neck, wore thick spectacles and made jerky little bows at us; he didn't smile or offer to shake hands. We watched the workmen surprisingly unearth a statue and a bronze bowl. Enrico whispered, "They put in last night"; but the unsuspecting Son of Heaven became quite excited and we left him chattering and hissing with his entourage.

264

On we walked through blazing streets, past wineshops and villas, courtyards and temples, all roofless under the glaring sky. It is an exhausting experience to visit Pompeii even on a cool day, but in the middle of July it is overpowering. I felt the stones burn through my shoes, and in the distance broken columns quivered through waves of heat. At last Enrico could go no farther. "I think now we send for chairs," he panted.

Our cars were waiting for us at the gate and beside them stood a young man. He stepped forward and said, "Signor Caruso, if I come to Sorrento will you give me an audition and tell me what you think of my voice?" I think I have never seen an expression as pitiful as Enrico's when he answered, "You want to sing? Yes, I will hear you. Come tomorrow morning." The boy, enraptured, said he would come at eleven. "Bring some music with you," Enrico called from the car.

At the hotel he went to bed at once, too exhausted to notice that Mario kept shaking his head and muttering, "Fools! What a shame!" That night I sat for a long time on the terrace, looking at the lights of Naples and dreading the morning.

I dressed before Enrico wakened. When he came out on the terrace he was paler than usual but said he had slept. "I go on no more excursions—it is enough," he said. We drank our coffee and waited for the boy.

I felt a shock when I saw that he had brought with him the score of *Martha*—I had expected some Neapolitan songs, not one of Enrico's best-loved operas.

"What voice you have—baritone?"

"No, Signor Caruso, tenor."

"So—you sing my part. Well, we try."

We went into the salon and Enrico seated himself at the

piano. "I know not to accompany—just some chords," he said. Neither his voice nor his eyes had any expression. I thought, "This is too horrible. How will he be able to stand it?"

"I will try to sing 'M'apparì,' " the boy said and Enrico struck a chord.

From the first note I knew that the boy had no voice. Enrico stopped him, told him not be nervous and to begin again. I went to my room to wait.

I heard them talking. The boy began again. I heard Enrico say, "No, no." There was a moment of silence.

And then I heard a voice! I ran to the salon. There stood Enrico, singing as he had never sung before. His voice was like a shower of stars, more beautiful than it had ever been. As he finished the song he flung out his arms. His face was transfigured. "Doro, I can sing! I can sing! I have not lost my voice. I can sing!"

Chapter Sixteen

USIC had come back into our lives. All that day, with an enthusiasm I had never heard from him before, Enrico talked of singing—not as hard work, a trust and a responsibility, but as a source of life and happiness.

That evening I sent Gloria's phonograph down to the hotel terrace and after dinner Enrico gave a concert of his records for the Ambassador and his wife. As that voice poured through the evening air people came silently from the salons and gardens to listen. He made little comments on his singing and hummed happily as he chose his songs. At midnight he sent Mario to fetch waltz and tango records, told everyone to dance and said good night.

In our room I watched him as he lay reading the newspaper and noticed that his eyes weren't following the printed lines. "Are you all right, Rico?" "Oh, yes," he answered, but he gave a little sigh. "I think on the time when Gloria will reach to the door handle. You know I don't mind to die, only I hate not to see our little girl grow up."

The next day we were delighted to learn that Giuseppe De Luca, baritone of the Metropolitan, was staying in Sorrento for the summer. He was a quiet good man whom we both liked very much. That afternoon he came to see us and had a long conversation with Enrico about the coming season and the great singers of the past. When he left Enrico said he would rest for an hour while I went down to the beach.

267

When I returned Mario met me at the door to say that Enrico had a visitor. I went to his room and found him lying down. An old, old man was bending over him. He held a probe in his hand and I saw that that hand was dirty.

"This is the doctor who took care of my dear mother," Enrico said.

"What is he doing with that probe?" I asked.

"I just show him my scars——"

"He should wash his hands before touching you."

"I know, but I not like to hurt his feelings, my Doro."

The old man didn't understand what we were saying and before I could stop him he lifted the little crust that I dressed so carefully each day and pushed his unsterilized probe into the old incision. "It is all healed but so much," he said, measuring off an inch on the probe with his dirty thumbnail.

The next morning Enrico looked feverish and I asked Nanny for a thermometer. He had a temperature of 101. The infection had started all over again.

I asked him to let me call a doctor, but he refused. He was restless and nervous and, worst of all, frightened. In desperation I sent for De Luca and told him what had happened. He said, "This may be very serious. We must get the Bastinelli brothers from Rome—they are the best doctors in Italy. This is how we will arrange: I will tell him I think you look badly, that you seem to be worried about him and that he should put your mind at rest by seeing these doctors." I agreed and he went in to see Enrico. An hour later they sent for me.

"My poor Doro," Enrico said, "Giuseppe say you worry for me. I will see doctors tomorrow and then you will be tranquil again."

The famous physicians arrived the next day. As they spoke perfect English I could tell them the complete history of Enrico's illness and show them the New York laboratory reports, as well as the daily record kept by Zirato.

I had expected their examination to take a long time, but in less than twenty minutes one of them came out on the terrace where I was waiting. In a low voice he said, "Madame Caruso, show no anxiety—your husband must have a kidney removed." I could only look at him, stunned. "But didn't you read the reports?" "Yes, but this is a new development. He must come to our clinic in Rome for the operation." "When?" "A week from Thursday." I said that I was afraid to wait a week, as his temperature was rising hourly. "Can't I bring him tomorrow?" I asked. "Next week will be time enough," he answered.

On Saturday night, suddenly, Enrico became delirious. He lay in bed, murmuring "*Sale, pepe—pepe, sale*" (salt, pepper—pepper, salt) over and over. Unless we could break the fever I was afraid that his heart would collapse. I asked Mario to bring a tumbler of whisky, and little by little Enrico managed to swallow it. In a few minutes he broke into such a violent sweat that the sheet clung to his entire body. His temperature began to fall and he slept.

In the night I decided that I could no longer, alone, take the responsibility for his life. I telephoned to his brother Giovanni in Naples that I refused to wait four days before taking Enrico to the clinic—that he was to engage a private train from Naples to Rome, reserve rooms in Naples at the Hotel Vesuvius, where we would stay overnight, and come at once to Sorrento to help us move.

Giovanni arrived early the next morning, Sunday, and we left for Naples by the noon boat.

Although in the hotel that night Enrico went to sleep with a temperature of 104, I found him sitting up in bed the next morning. He asked for Gloria, played with her for a few minutes, then kissed her and let her go.

It was the first of August and Naples was deserted. I stood on the balcony outside our windows, in the white burning glare of the bay, and watched a boy eat a watermelon. "It is a good fruit," Enrico said, "you eat, you drink and you wash your face." A herd of goats passed by in the street below, then a lemon vendor and his song.

Inside the air was cooler. "I will close the curtains and perhaps you can sleep," I was saying when, without warning, Enrico's eyes fixed on me with a startled stare and he screamed. Instantly Mario raced past the door, crying, "I will find a doctor."

It was like Christmas Day. Enrico shrieked with every breath he drew. This time I had no ether and while waiting I could only hold him in my arms and wipe his poor dripping face. . . . Mario came back to report that all the bellboys had been sent out to find doctors but that most of them had left the city for the summer holidays. The frightened manager rushed up to tell me that all the hospitals had been notified, that surely some doctor would soon be found. . . . But no one came.

After an hour Enrico sounded like a tortured animal—his voice was no longer human. His screams became long howls and I think no one ever suffered such agony.

Two more hours passed and still no doctor could be found. I begged Giovanni to bring in a dentist, a nurse, a veterinary— anyone who might have access to morphine and a needle. It was inconceivable that in a great city like Naples, where Caruso was worshiped, not a single person could be found to come to our rescue in this desperate crisis.

Enrico had screamed for four hours before the first doctor arrived—and he had brought no morphine! When he returned with it his hand trembled so with fright that he couldn't make the injection. I took the syringe and did it for him. In ten minutes the screams stopped and Enrico fell into a stupor.

Then, one after another, six more doctors arrived. They examined Enrico, then went into the salon to confer. When they sent for me an hour later I found them seated around the big table. They told me that they proposed to remove the left kidney that night, but dared not give complete anesthesia because his heart wouldn't stand the strain. If they operated he would live two weeks in terrible pain, and at the end of that time his chance of living was only one in a thousand; but on the other hand, if they didn't operate he would die before morning. It was I who must make the decision.

I turned to Enrico's brother. "Giovanni, what shall I do?" He was holding a handkerchief against his mouth and crying. Without replying he bowed his head and sobbed aloud.

I said to the doctors, "They saved him in America—why can't you?" But they only shook their heads and waited.

At last I said, "Of course it must be done. But before you start the kidney operation I ask you first to open the lower incision in his side, under the little scar. Go in four inches and with your fingers feel for an abscess the size of a walnut. Break it and insert a drain—in twenty-four hours he will be out of danger. I will take all the responsibility. If you don't find the abscess, then you can operate on the kidney."

They asked me to leave them while they discussed my decision. After an hour they called me back and announced that it was useless to operate at all.

I pleaded with them with all my strength to probe for the abscess, but they refused. I beat at them desperately with my arguments, but they seemed not to hear—it was as if a plate-glass window stood between us, shutting out my voice. "At least give him a blood transfusion," I begged. This they also refused. All

271

they would consent to do was to send for a tank of oxygen.

In spite of what they said I could not believe that he was near death. With every part of my being I concentrated on his living, as I had done through that long night in New York. . . .

He looked strange and gray in the dawn, as I knelt beside him with my hand against his cheek. Hours passed. . . .

The doctor beside me lifted his wrist to count the pulse. I heard the wall clock striking nine and the sound of water being poured into a glass. He opened his eyes and looked at me.

"Doro—I—am—thirsty——" He gave a little cough. "Doro—they—hurt—me—again." He began to gasp for air.

"Don't be afraid, Rico darling—everything is all right."

"Doro—I—can't—get—my—breath——"

I saw his eyes close and his hand drop. I hid my face and thought, "At last Enrico is well." I wanted to go out in the sunlight but knew I could not because no one would understand. From far away came sounds of weeping and two nuns entered, murmuring prayers. I rose from my knees and walked out of the door without looking back.

Chapter Seventeen

I wENT into the next room and lay down. Brunetta was there and tried not to let me see that she was crying. A procession of weeping people began to pass from Enrico's room into mine and stopped to look at me. They didn't speak, and I didn't know who they were. Then a priest sat down beside me and asked if there was anything he could do. He said he had known Enrico for many years and loved him very much.

The next morning Baroness Romano Avezzana came from Sorrento to help me. She went to the shops and returned with a long heavy crepe veil—until then I hadn't thought about mourning. I told her that Enrico was no longer in his room but downstairs in the salon of the hotel; that I hadn't found the courage to see him again, and how this had shocked and angered Giovanni. I said nothing was real, I couldn't even cry and the Italians thought I was cold and without feeling. The Baroness understood and answered in a natural voice that she would go down to see him and then tell me what I ought to do. She came back to say that he was surrounded by beautiful flowers and looked as if he were quietly sleeping: but she felt sure he would prefer that I remember him as he had always been, full of life and singing.

All Naples was talking, she said, about the King's offer of the Royal Basilica of the Church of San Francisco di Paola for the funeral—a unique tribute, as only funerals for members of the royal family had ever been held there. I alone in all the city could not feel the weight and glory of this solemn honor. There had been many kings, but only one Caruso. Although I knew that he was lying in state downstairs and that crowds were filing by to look at him for the last time, I could not believe that he would never again come smiling into a room saying, "Ah, you are there, my Doro." I waited and waited to wake from this incredible dream.

* * *

The life of the city stopped on the day of the funeral. Flags hung at half mast; the shops were closed, covered with crepe and signs—LUTTO PER CARUSO. At eleven o'clock the great bell began to toll, and for the first time I went out into the living world without Enrico. His stepmother, brother and elder son were waiting for me and we drove through a glare of white buildings that shone dimly through the dusk of my veil. I sat in the carriage in desolate isolation and watched the others weep.

Two walls of soldiers held back a dense crowd in the big square before the church. As I left the carriage two soldiers came forward and preceded me up the steps. The great wooden doors at the top were closed. The soldiers beat on them with the butts of their muskets, and as they swung slowly open the crowd shouted, "Make way for the widow! Make way for the widow!"

Inside the church thousands and thousands of faces turned toward me. At the end of the long aisle, before the altar rail, stood a high catafalque covered with flowers. On the top, very far away from me, I saw a small coffin. The organ was playing. I walked up the aisle toward my place within the sanctuary and the high Requiem Mass began. . . .

When I came out of the church the bright sun blinded me and a stranger took my arm to help me down the steps. Giovanni struck at his hand and shouted so that all might hear, "You have taken my brother from me—will you take my sister also?" He burst into tears and covered his face with a large black-bordered handkerchief. In the carriage on the way to the cemetery he stopped weeping and wiped his red face and the inside of his hat. His stepmother said, "Stop acting," and they began to quarrel viciously.

The green and flowering cemetery of Del Planto lies on the outskirts of Naples. It was there, in a chapel lent to us until his own could be built, that I left Enrico.

* * *

I didn't return to the Hotel Vesuvius but went directly to the quiet Bertellini, high above the city, where Mario, Brunetta and Nanny were waiting. Baby met me at the door. She had two tiny black bows pinned on the shoulders of her little white frock.

It was good to see a sweep of sky and water from the wide uncovered terrace, and to hear no voices except those of my dear servants and my baby. In the evenings Brunetta sat near me and sewed; she didn't speak unless I spoke first. Mario served my meals in one of the small salons. A little mouse lived in this room and as I ate I threw crumbs to him. I wanted him to come close enough to eat out of my hand and each night I placed the crumbs nearer and nearer my chair; but he would come only a little way and then run back into his hole. . . . I was lost but not lonely.

* * *

Days passed before I received an answer to my question: what was the real cause of Enrico's death? But at last I learned that he had not died of an infected kidney but of peritonitis, due to the bursting of an abscess at the place I had indicated. The operation for which I had pleaded might have saved his life.

It seemed useless to discuss with the Bastinellis the diagnosis they had made in Sorrento—I realized that doctors are not infallible. As for those in Naples, their ignorance of the case and

275

the eminence of the patient had so frightened them that they hadn't dared take the responsibility for the consequences of an emergency operation.

* * *

In my bitter and defeated grief I didn't speak of Enrico at all, and I longed to close my mind to all memories. Yet day after day I sat at my desk for hours to answer the messages of a sorrowing world. They came from Alexandra of England, from Samuel Gompers of New York, from a newsboy in Chicago and a shepherd in Scotland—from thousands of the multitude that had loved his divine voice. One message came from Germany and said simply, "I am coming." It was signed "Schol."

For many days he didn't appear and then one morning he was waiting in the salon. He told me he had left Munich the day Enrico died but had been arrested at the border. He was carrying with him his life savings of five thousand dollars and had no idea that he wasn't allowed to take this money out of the country. Nevertheless, the Germans put him in prison, took everything away from him, and now he possessed nothing but the suit he was wearing.

He told his story in a few words, then paused. "Can I see him?" he asked at last. I said gently that I wouldn't go with him and explained that he would find Enrico lying under a shelter of glass as though asleep. He thanked me and left for the cemetery.

When he came back he stood before me on the terrace and looked at the sky. After a long pause he spoke.

"I leaned over and whispered to him, 'Don't you know poor old Schol?' But he did not answer me."

That was all he said, but at last I was able to cry.

Before he left I arranged for him to stay on in Naples and told him I would take him back with me to America.

* * *

In September I went to Signa. For the first time since Enrico's death I was free of Italian relatives, bankers and lawyers and could make my plans for returning home.

Martino showed me the flowers Enrico had chosen in New York from the seed catalogue. Now they were in full bloom outside my window. I visited the kitchens and pantries, storerooms and wine cellars and all the silent rooms of the villa. Everything was in perfect order. I unpacked the linen we had ordered from the little shop in Sorrento. I covered the little figures of the unfinished crèche and put away the music he had left on the piano.

I knew that one day I would have to hear his voice again on a record. The thought that it might come from a strange house, through an open window, was unbearable—I could prepare myself for this anguish only by first facing it here, and alone. One afternoon I sent all the servants out of the villa and went to the music room. I chose one of the gayest of his songs, "*Luna d'estate*," and put it on the victrola. Once again his voice was in the room, but I sat listening almost without recognition, my heart locked in ice, until I saw Gloria stumbling through the doorway, holding out her arms and calling, "Daddy! Daddy!"

My interviews with the head farmer, the administrator, the appointed guardians of Gloria, and all the business and inventories of Enrico's vast estate were finished. It was time now to leave Italy. Mario told me that he and Brunetta would like to go to France and take care of me until I sailed. He never wanted to valet anyone else after Enrico and he planned to look for a position in some shop in Florence. I said I thought it would be nicer for Brunetta if he had his own shop—so I gave it to him and he was glad.

* * *

Old Schol was waiting for us in Le Havre. As the boat was about to sail Mario said, "Signora, Brunetta and I have one last favor to ask of you." I thought, "What have I left undone?" and promised to grant the favor if I could. He took Brunetta's hand and they smiled at me. "May we make a baby now?" From far away came the picture of Enrico sitting at his desk, giving them permission to marry at last, but with the warning, "No babies!"

Each morning Schol came to my deck chair, made a grave little bow and asked if I felt well. He was wearing a coat of Enrico's I had given him. It touched the ground and the sleeves hung to his knees, but he was unconscious of his curious appearance—he was clothed in a memory.

Chapter Eighteen

GLORIA and I arrived in New York on a bright October morning. Zirato was the first to reach us on deck and, as in former days, stood beside me while reporters and photographers gathered around us, asking the familiar questions. These men had been such a part of Enrico's life that they brought a sudden warmth to my bleak home-coming. He had always said, "It is not just for me that I talk to the boys of the newspapers. They work hard to make the pictures and write the story. That is how they live—like me singing." So I answered all their questions, posed with Gloria and did as he used to do.

I went to live at the St. Regis because it was near Central Park, where the baby could go to play. She was nearly two, and the park was a fabulous land. Every afternoon she returned with tales of wondrous talking squirrels and sailing swans, and of how Chick the policeman stopped all the cars to take her and Nanny across the street. She gathered rich treasures of red balloons and bright autumn leaves and brought them to the room where I sat without a future, trying to make a friend of an unknown world of dim outline.

There was little secretarial work for Zirato to do now, but it comforted me to hear the click of his typewriter in the next room. One morning he brought me a box of Enrico's papers and among them we found a list of people in Italy whom he had supported for years. Besides the scores of relatives, the list included a hundred and twenty men and women who had shown him some small kindness in the past which he had never forgotten. He had never mentioned these gifts, any more than he had ever spoken of the other countless good deeds which were a natural part of his daily life.

Until now I hadn't realized how much Enrico had protected me from people. During our three years together I had seen them only through his eyes, and as if from distance. Now they were near, large and out of focus. I wanted time and space and silence in which to place my thoughts like slow careful steps that follow each other in a straight line; but the kindness and curiosity of people made this impossible. As the king of singers, Enrico had belonged to them as much as to me; therefore I was expected to behave, not as an unhappy young widow, but as a bereaved queen. Everyone talked about the world's loss of the singer; no one but myself knew the elemental splendor of the man or the unearthly quality of the love we had given each other.

In the beginning, when I was asked to tell about our life together, I responded eagerly and to anyone. With my words I seemed to see him, and for a little while I was not alone. But they had soon heard enough; their eyes wandered, and when I paused they spoke of other things. Then I would continue in a kind of desperation, hoping they would understand why they must listen and in that way help save something that was my life but that I could not explain. At last I stopped. I began to understand why Enrico had wanted me to keep away from people and give my confidence to no one.

* * *

In the summer I went back to Naples to see his tomb. It lay in a lovely chapel of white stone in the shade of cypress trees. Above the altar, watching over the white marble sarcophagus, stood our gentle Madonna of a thousand prayers.

I didn't approach the sarcophagus, for I did not want to see

280

Enrico. Although I had asked to have the casket covered, his family had refused—it was the Italian custom to display the bodies of their great dead. But visitors from other countries where this custom did not obtain found such a display shocking. It wasn't until eight years later, when I made an appeal directly to the government through Prince Barberini, that I succeeded in having the sarcophagus closed.

* * *

The one person in the world who knew how I felt about Enrico was Jacqueline Romano Avezzana, and during the years that followed his death I went every spring to visit her at the Italian Embassy in Paris. She and her husband had become my closest friends and we spent our summers together in Venice. One autumn before I went back to America, Jacqueline spoke to me about marrying again. Since I was only thirty-one, she saw lonely years ahead for Gloria and me, without protection and companionship.

The next spring she died. There was a poignant irony in being able to offer to her family some measure of the comfort and help she had so compassionately given me in Naples when Enrico died.

In my new loneliness I decided to follow her advice and re-marry. Unhappily the marriage was a failure, but from it came the one thing Gloria longed for—a sister. She was born in New York and I named her in memory of my dead friend.

As I had given Signa to Enrico's family,* I decided to estab-

* The Villa Bellosguardo and its many farms at Signa were too difficult for me to administer for Gloria until she should become of age.

The greater part of Enrico's art collections is in the care of his old valet, Martino. Since the war I have had no news of them.

I have given some of his costumes to various singers. I have never parted with the white cashmere costume which he wore in *Pagliacci*.

King Victor Emmanuel bought Enrico's ancient gold coins to add to his own collection.

lish my home in New York. I bought a house and tried to find my place in the normal modern life that seemed to satisfy everyone else. After a month I knew this was impossible. My lovely house became a prison. I would return to it, after a brilliant party, and the moment the front door closed behind me I was shut into the silence of my lost world. My state was beyond loneliness and longing; it was the silence of emptiness and unreality.

When this feeling became overpowering I would cancel all my engagements and sail for Europe with Nanny and the children. Often I would go first to the little town of Sorrento, and from the same terrace where Enrico and I had lived so confidently I would watch the night come down upon the sea. I bought linen again from the same little shop, and ordered Gloria's wedding veil to be made by the same nuns.

Twelve years had passed since Enrico's death. Gloria was thirteen and Jacqueline seven. Again I was being urged to marry —this time by my family as well as my friends—so that my children might grow up in the security of an established conventional life.

Again I listened and again I failed. I don't think these failures were anyone's fault. Death had not ended my marriage to Enrico. Any other human being was as unsubstantial as a shadow in comparison to his continuous reality. When I tried to make the shadow real the situation became impossible for both of us.

* * *

It is now twenty-three years since he died, but I still receive letters from strangers who loved him and have never forgotten. They send me little stories of how they met him, or how he made a caricature of them once upon a time; they ask me to confirm some legend they have heard about him, or offer me a souvenir they have treasured. Since the war many have inquired about his tomb. The other day I received a letter from Naples, from an American soldier whom I do not know:

"The name Caruso is an intimate part of this city. The first day I went sight-seeing, as we went into the Cathedral of San Francisco di Paolo the guide told us that Caruso's funeral had been held there. Later in the week I found a sergeant to take me in his command car out to the cemetery where we searched for Caruso's tomb. A gentle rain was falling, it was late afternoon, the cemetery was quiet—it was a memorable occasion for both of us when the guide brought us to the lovely white mausoleum and announced proudly: 'Caruso.'

"After paying our silent tribute to the memory of the great man, the sergeant and I trudged back up the hill in the rain, each in his own way giving thanks that the war had not erased all the shrines, both great and small, which men have erected to recall the past and give inspiration to the future."

* * *

More than half my life has been lived in the memory of three brief years—those years which at first I struggled desperately to forget, then only to remember.

This book has been finished on his birthday—he would be seventy-one today. I have been sitting by the radio, listening to his voice singing gloriously on a memorial program. He would have liked this tribute. He would have said, "So kind of them to remember, after so long."

New York, February 25, 1944

APPENDIX

High Points in Caruso's Life

Enrico Caruso was born February 27, 1873, in Naples at No. 7 Via San Giovannello agli Otto Calli.

He made his official debut in Naples at the Nuova in *L'Amico Francesco,* November 16, 1894.

He made his debut in New York at the Metropolitan in *Rigoletto,* November 23, 1903.

He made his first Victor record, "La donna è mobile" from *Rigoletto,* February 1, 1904.

He made his last record, Rossini's "Messe Solennelle," September 14, 1920.

He gave his last performance at the Metropolitan in *La Juive,* December 24, 1920.

He died in Naples at the Hotel Vesuvius, August 2, 1921.

He sang in: Italy, Russia, Germany, France, Belgium, Portugal, Spain, Monaco, Austria, Hungary, Czechoslovakia, England, Ireland, Scotland, Argentina, Brazil, Uruguay, Mexico, Cuba, Canada and the United States.

He spoke Italian, English, French, German, Spanish, Portuguese and Russian.

He sang *Pagliacci* 76 times, and *Aïda* 64 times, at the Metropolitan.

His last performance was the 607th he had sung at the Metropolitan.

He was paid $960 a performance the first year he sang there, $1152 the second, $1344 the third, $1440 the fourth. (During these years he was paid in francs—5000, 6000, 7000 and 7500.) After that he received $2000 a performance until the opening of the 1914–15 season when his old contract expired. For his new contract he was asked to name the sum to which he felt entitled, up to $4000. He did not take advantage of this offer but replied that $2500 was enough. More than that would place him under an obligation of driving himself to greater efforts, and the quality of his performance would suffer. Until his death, seven years later, he continued to receive only $2500 a performance.

Operatic Repertoire

* Adriana Lecouvreur, by Cilèa
L'Africana, by Meyerbeer
Aïda, by Verdi
L'Amico Francesco, by Morelli
L'Amore dei tre re, by Monte-
  mezzi
* L'Arlesiana, by Cilèa
Armide, by Gluck
A San Francisco, by Sebastiani
Un Ballo in Maschera, by Verdi
La Bohème, by Puccini
La Bohème, by Leoncavallo
Camoëns, by Musoni
Carmen, by Bizet
Cavalleria rusticana, by Mascagni
Celeste, by Marengo
Don Giovanni, by Mozart
Don Pasquale, by Donizetti
Un Dramma in Vendemmia, by
  Fornari
Il Duca d'Alba, by Donizetti
L'Elisir d'Amore, by Donizetti
* La Fanciulla del West, by Puc-
  cini
Faust, by Gounod
La Favorita, by Donizetti
* Fedora, by Giordano
La Forza del destino, by Verdi
Fra Diavolo, by Auber
* Germania, by Franchetti
La Gioconda, by Ponchielli
Il Guarany, by Gomes
Guglielmo Tell, by Rossini
Hedda, by Leborne
Les Huguenots, by Meyerbeer
Iris, by Mascagni

La Juive, by Halévy
Julien, by Charpentier
Jupanki, by Berutti
Lodoletta, by Mascagni
Lohengrin, by Wagner
Lucia di Lammermoor, by Doni-
  zetti
Lucrezia Borgia, by Donizetti
Madama Butterfly, by Puccini
The Magic Flute, by Mozart
Malia, by Frontini
Manon, by Massenet
Manon Lescaut, by Puccini
Maria di Rohan, by Donizetti
Mariedda, by Bucceri
Martha, by Flotow
* Le Maschere, by Mascagni
Mefistofele, by Boïto
Navarraise, by Massenet
Otello, by Verdi
Pagliacci, by Leoncavallo
Les Pecheurs de Perles, by Bizet
Profeta di Korasan, by Napoli-
  tano
Le Prophète, by Meyerbeer
I Puritani, by Bellini
Regina di Saba, by Goldmark
Rigoletto, by Verdi
Romeo e Giulietta, by Gounod
Samson et Dalila, by Saint-Saëns
Sapho, by Massenet
La Sonnambula, by Donizetti
Tosca, by Puccini
La Traviata, by Verdi
Il Trovatore, by Verdi
Il Voto, by Giordano

* World premières.

Caruso Recordings

A DISCOGRAPHY

THE EARLIEST recordings by Enrico Caruso were issued in Europe by the Pathé and the Zonophone Companies, some time between 1898 and 1901, though the exact dates are impossible to determine now. The first Pathé records, made in France, were cylindrical, though they were also later issued on flat Pathé discs. These discs were cut vertically ("hill-and-dale") instead of laterally, as all modern commercial discs are cut, and can therefore be played only on Pathé phonographs or on machines equipped with the correct needle and a reversible reproducer. Both the cylinders and the discs issued by Pathé are listed below. They were sold in Italy by the Anglo-Italian Commerce Company of Genoa, and there seems to have been some arrangement between Pathé and the Anglo-Italian Commerce Company for their distribution in other countries.

In 1902 Caruso began recording for the Gramophone and Typewriter Company of England, later much better known as H.M.V. (His Master's Voice), an affiliate of Victor. The Zonophone recordings reveal a much lighter, more lyrical quality in Caruso's voice than those made for the Gramophone and Typewriter Company, and the latter, in turn, are lighter and more lyrical than those made still later for the Victor Company in the United States.

Shortly after Caruso's debut, November 23, 1903, at the Metropolitan Opera House in *Rigoletto*, he was engaged to make records for the Victor Company. His first recording for that company was *Questa o quella* from the same opera, Victor record No. 81025, and it was made in the early part of February, 1904. From that time on, Caruso confined his recording work to the Victor Company in the United States and the affiliated companies in Europe.

Despite the fact that many other labels will be found, the discography below includes all the original recordings Caruso ever made. The reasons for the variety of labels are two: First, the companies affiliated with Victor throughout the world issued Caruso records under various makes and labels, but they were pressed from the original masters. Second, there were many pirate editions put on the market at one time, all of them copies of either the domestic Victor Company or of the affiliated companies in Europe. The masters were almost all made by Victor in Camden, N. J.; the rest were made by H.M.V. in England. The better known pirates were the Opera Disc and Pan-American Records. In the early 20's, the Victor Company began legal action against firms making such copies of the Caruso records and their manufacture was soon stopped.

During the past few years the Victor Company has re-issued many of the earlier Caruso recordings both as originally released in the mechanical or acoustical type of recording and with new electrically recorded orchestral accompaniments. Re-issues of the early Gramophone and Typewriter records can also be obtained from England, such records being listed in the No. 2 (Historical) Section of the standard H.M.V. catalogue.

VALUES OF CARUSO RECORDS

Older Caruso recordings are heavily in demand both by collectors of great voices of the past and by students of vocal art. The prices such records bring are determined both by their rarity and by the condition in which they are. Accordingly, the highest prices are those paid for Zonophone records which, when they are in excellent condition, may bring as much as $100 each. Pathé cylinders range from $25 to $50; Pathé discs usually bring about $25. The Gramophone and Typewriter records range from $5 to $10, depending on rarity, while the 5000 Victor series (pressed here from European masters) average $10. This 5000 series was also later renumbered as a 91,000 series.

Early Victor releases had various labels. The Monarch labels (10-inch records) and the De Luxe labels (12-inch records) vary in price from $3 to $10; Grand Prize labels (both 10 and 12-inch records), from $2.50 to $5. All later series of 10-inch records, with very few exceptions, are valued from $1 to $1.50 for single-faced records and

$2 to $2.50 for doubles, while 12-inch records are $2 for singles, $3.50 for doubles. These later records, however, have to be in either excellent or unused condition.

The following abbreviations are used to indicate record brands and makes:

C.R.S.–Collectors Record Shop
E–Emerson
G&T–Gramophone and Type-
    writer
HMV–His Master's Voice

IRCC–International Record Col-
    lectors' Club
P–Pathé
V–Victor
ZON–Zonophone

The numbers immediately following the brand abbreviations indicate the size of the record. For example, V 10 87312 means Victor Record, 10-inch, No. 87312. Figures in the column headed "doubled with" refer to the numbers preceding each title in the first column, and indicate the selection on the other side of each record. Thus, selection 1 is doubled with 35, and also with 153, which means that one record (number 502) contains *Addio a Napoli* on one side and *Canta pe'me* on the reverse; and another record (number 2212) contains *Addio a Napoli* on one side and *Musica proibita* on the reverse. Figures in the "date recorded" column refer to month and year. Thus 9/19 means September, 1919.

JACK L. CAIDIN

Collectors Record Shop
New York City

TITLE AND COMPOSER †INDICATES RECORDS STILL IN PRINT	DOU-BLED WITH	DATE RE-CORDED	MAKE, SIZE AND 1ST NO.	LATER NOS.
† 1. Addio a Napoli, T. *Cottrau*	35 153	9/19	V 10 87312	502 2212
2. Adorables Tourments, *Barthelemy* (French)	46	1/08	V 12 88115	6006
ADRIANA LECOUVREUR, *Cilea:* 3. –No più nobile (piano-Cilea)		11/02	G&T 10 52419	
AFRICANA, *Meyerbeer:* 4. –Deh', ch'io ritorni	96	9/20	V 12 7156	
† 5. –O Paradiso	39 39	12/06	V 12 88054	6007 14234
† 6. Agnus Dei (Latin), *Bizet*	148 100	3/12	V 12 88425	6010 17814
7. A Granada (Spanish), *Alvarez* [also issued on 10-inch later]	33 17 156 156	9/18	V 12 88623	6011 8038 17-5001 26571
AIDA, *Verdi:* 8 –Celeste Aïda (piano)		3/02	G&T 10 52369	matrix no.1784
9. –Celeste Aïda (piano) [also issued in U. S., 5008, 91007]		1903	G&T 10 52369	matrix no.2873
10. –Celeste Aïda (piano)		2/04	V 12 85022	
11. –Celeste Aïda (without Recit.)		3/08	V 12 88127	
†12. –Celeste Aïda (with Recit.)	82 171*	12/11	V 12 88127	6000 7770 8993
13. –La fatal pietra (with Gadski)	14	11/09	V 12 89028	8015
14. –O terra, addio (with Gadski)	13	11/09	V 12 89029	8015
15. –Aïda a me togliesti (with Homer)	16	12/10	V 12 89051	8012
16. –Già i sacerdoti (with Homer)	15	12/10	V 12 89050	8012
17. A la luz de la luna (Spanish; with de Gogorza), *Michelena*	7	4/18	V 12 89083	8038
18. Alba separa dalla luce l'ombra, *Tosti*	150	4/17	V 10 87272	503
AMADIS, *Lully:* 19. –Bois épais (French)	178	9/20	V 10 1437	
20. Amore mio, *Ricciardi*	48	1/14	V 10 87176	504
ANDREA CHENIER, *Giordano:* 21. –Come un bel dì	45	11/16	V 10 87266	516
22. –Un dì all'azzurro spazio	40	3/07	V 12 88060	6008
†23. Ave Maria (Latin; piano– Kahn; violin–Elman), *Kahn*	59	3/13	V 12 89065	8007
24. Bacio ancora (piano), *Trimarchi*		1902	ZON 10 1550	
†25. Because (French), *D'Hardelot*	99 150	12/12	V 10 87122	506 1688

*Also with Victor 8993: Ponselle–Aïda–Ritorna.

TITLE AND COMPOSER †INDICATES RECORDS STILL IN PRINT	DOU-BLED WITH	DATE RE-CORDED	MAKE, SIZE AND 1ST NO.	LATER NOS.
BOHEME, Leoncavallo:				
26. –Io non ho che una povera stanzetta	27	11/11	V 12 88335	6012
27. –Testa adorata	26	11/11	V 12 88331	6012
BOHEME, Puccini:				
28. –Che gelida manina	110	2/06	V 12 88002	6003
29. –O soave fanciulla (with Farrar) (never released on regular issue)	170	12/12	IRCC 12 61	
30. –O soave fanciulla (with Melba)		3/07	V 12 95200	
†31. –O Mimì, tu più (with Scotti)	86	3/07	V 12 89006	8000
†32. -Quartet (with Farrar, Viafora Scotti)	* 193	3/08	V 12 96002	10007 16-5001
33. Campana di San Giusto, Arona	7	1/19	V 12 88612	6011
34. Campane a Sera (originally Spanish song; Italian version by Caruso), Malfetti	174	9/18	V 12 88615	6024
35. Canta pe'me, De Curtis	1	11/11	V 10 87092	502
36. Cantique de Noël (French), Adam	199	2/16	V 12 88561	6029
CARMEN, Bizet:				
37. –Flower Song (Italian; piano)		2/05	V 12 85049	
38. –Flower Song (French)	68	11/09	V 12 88208	6004
†39. –Flower Song (Italian)	55	11/09	V 12 88209	6007 14234
CAVALLERIA, Mascagni:				
†40. –Addio alla madre	22 181	12/13	V 12 88458	6008 15732
41. –Brindisi (piano)	44	2/05	V 10 81062	521
42. –Siciliana (piano)		1902	ZON 10 1556	
43. –Siciliana (piano) [also issued in United States, 5012, 91011]		11/02	G&T 10 52418	
44. –Siciliana (piano)	41	2/04	V 10 81030	521
45. –Siciliana (harp)	21	12/10	V 10 87072	516
46. Chanson de Juin (French), Godard	2	11/16	V 12 88579	6006
CID, Massenet:				
47. –O Souverain (French)	107	2/16	V 12 88554	6013
48. Cielo turchino, Ciociano	20	1/15	V 10 87218	504
49. Core 'ngrato, Cardillo	200	11/11	V 12 88334	6032
50. Crucifix (French; with Journet), Faure	§	1/12	V 12 89054	6347
51. Danza, Rossini	210	2/12	V 12 88355	6031

*Also with Victor 10007: Farrar and Scotti–Bohème.
§ With Victor 6347: Plançon–Rameaux.

TITLE AND COMPOSER †INDICATES RECORDS STILL IN PRINT	DOU-BLED WITH	DATE RE-CORDED	MAKE, SIZE AND 1ST NO.	LATER NOS.
52. Deux Sérénades (French; piano —Scognamiglio; violin—Elman), Leoncavallo	207	2/15	V 12 89085	8008
DON CARLOS, Verdi:				
53. —Dio che nell'alma (with Scotti)	172	12/12	V 12 89064	8036
DON PASQUALE, Donizetti:				
54. —Com' è gentil (piano)	94	2/05	V 12 85048	6036
DON SEBASTIANO, Donizetti:				
55. —In terra solo	121	1/08	V 12 88106	6014
†56. Dream (English), Bartlett	81 81	9/20	V 10 87321	507 1658
57. Dreams of long ago (English), Carroll-Caruso	114	4/12	V 12 88376	6015
DUCA D'ALBA, Donizetti:				
58. —Angelo casto e bel	97	1/15	V 12 88516	6355
†59. Elégie (French; piano—Kahn; violin—Elman), Massenet	23	3/13	V 12 89066	8007
ELISIR D'AMORE, Donizetti:				
60. —Una furtiva lagrima (piano)		1902	ZON 10 1552	
61. —Una furtiva lagrima (piano)		3/02	G&T 10 52346	
62. —Una furtiva lagrima (piano; part 1)	164	2/04	V 10 81027	930
63. —Una furtiva lagrima (piano; part 2)		2/04	V 12 85021	
†64. —Una furtiva lagrima (orch.)	188 188	12/11	V 12 88339	6016 11-8112
65. —Venti scudi (with DeLuca)	85	2/19	V 12 89089	8006
66. Eternamente, Mascheroni	196	11/11	V 12 88333	6034
EUGENE ONEGIN, Tschaikowsky:				
67. —Air de Lenski (French)	154	11/16	V 12 88582	6017
FAUST, Gounod:				
68. —Salut! demeure (French)	38	2/06	V 12 88003	6004
69. —Attends, voici la rue (French; with Farrar)	72	1/10	V 12 89034	8010
70. —Eternelle (French; with Farrar)	71	1/10	V 12 89031	8009
71. —Laisse-moi (French; with Farrar)	70	1/10	V 12 89032	8009
72. —Mon coeur (French; with Farrar)	69	1/10	V 12 89033	8010
†73. —Alerte, ou vous êtes perdus (French; with Farrar and Journet)	198*	1/10	V 12 95203	10008 16-5003
74. —Trio du duel (French; with Scotti and Journet)	192	1/10	V 12 95206	10011

*Also with Victor 10008: Farrar and Journet—Faust—Elle ouvre.

TITLE AND COMPOSER †INDICATES RECORDS STILL IN PRINT	DOU-BLED WITH	DATE RE-CORDED	MAKE, SIZE AND 1ST NO.	LATER NOS.
75. −Seigneur Dieu (French; with Farrar, Mme. Gilibert, Journet)	76	1/10	V 12 95204	10004
76. −Eh quoi toujours seule (French; with Farrar, Mme. Gilibert, Journet)	75	1/10	V 12 95205	10004
77. −O merveille (French; with Journet)	134	1/10	V 12 89039	8016
FAVORITA, Donizetti:				
78. −Spirito gentil	102	2/06	V 12 88004	6005
FEDORA, Giordano:				
79. −Amor ti vieta (piano— Giordano)		11/02	G&T 10 52439	
80. Fenesta che lucive, Composer unknown	104	4/13	V 12 88439	6019
†81. For you alone (English), Geehl	56 56	12/10	V 10 87070	507 1658
FORZA DEL DESTINO, Verdi:				
†82. −O tu che in seno agli angeli	12	11/09	V 12 88207	6000
83. −Invano Alvaro (with Amato)	84	11/11	V 12 89052	8005
84. −Le minaccie (with Amato)	83	11/11	V 12 89053	8005
85. −Il segreto (with DeLuca)	65	7/18	V 12 89087	8006
†86. −Solenne in quest'ora (with Scotti)	31	3/06	V 12 89001	8000
87. Garibaldi's Hymn, Mercantini	161	9/18	V 10 87297	515
GERMANIA, Franchetti:				
88. −Non chiuder gli occhi (piano)		1902	ZON 10 1554	
89. −Non chiuder gli occhi (piano)		3/02	G&T 10 52370	
90. −Non chiuder gli occhi (orch.)	92	3/10	V 10 87054	508
91. −Studenti, udite (piano)		3/02	G&T 10 52378	
92. −Studenti, udite (orchestra)	90	3/10	V 10 87053	508
GIOCONDA, Ponchielli:				
93. −Cielo e mar (piano) [also issued in United States, 5009, 91008]		11/02	G&T 10 52417	
94. −Cielo e mar (piano)	54	2/05	V 12 85055	6036
95. −Cielo e mar (orchestra)	127	3/10	V 12 88246	6020
96. Goodbye (Addio), Tosti	153 4	12/10	V 12 88280	6021 7156
GUARANY, Gomez:				
97. −Sento una forza indomita (with Destinn)	58	4/14	V 12 89078	6355
98. Guardann' a Luna, Crescenzo	109	4/13	V 10 87162	509
99. Hantise d'amour (French), Szulc	25	3/14	V 10 87211	506
†100. Hosanna (French), Granier	182 6	12/12	V 12 88403	6022 17814

TITLE AND COMPOSER †INDICATES RECORDS STILL IN PRINT	DOU-BLED WITH	DATE RE-CORDED	MAKE, SIZE AND 1ST NO.	LATER NOS.
HUGUENOTS, *Meyerbeer:*				
101. −Bianca al par (piano)		2/05	V 12 85056	
102. −Bianca al par	78	11/09	V 12 88210	6005
†103. −Quì sotto il ciel (piano)		1898-99	P 14 84006	
Also on Pathé cylinders				
Also re-issued on regular cut	229		C.R.S. 10 6	
C.R.S.	C.R.S.			
104. Ideale, *Tosti*	80	12/06	V 12 88049	6019
105. I' m' arricordo e Napule, *Gioe*	125	9/20	V 12 88635	6009
IRIS, *Mascagni:*				
106. −Serenata (piano)		3/02	G&T 10 52368	
JUIVE, *Halévy:*				
107. −Rachel, quand du Seigneur (French)	47	9/20	V 12 88625	6013
†108. Largo from Xerxes, *Händel*	112	1/20	V 12 88617	6023
[re-recorded with organ]	112			8806
109. Lasciati amar, *Leoncavallo*	98	4/13	V 10 87161	509
110. Lolita, *Buzzi-Peccia*	28	3/08	V 12 88120	6003
LOMBARDI, *Verdi:*				
†111. −Qual volutta (with Alda and Journet)	198	1/12	V 12 95211	10010
	137			16-5002
†112. Lost Chord (English), *Sullivan*	108	5/12	V 12 88378	6023
[re-recorded with organ]	108			8806
113. Love is mine (English), *Gartner*	166	12/11	V 10 87095	510
114. Love me or not (English), *Secchi*	57	1/20	V 12 88616	6015
LUCIA, *Donizetti:*				
115. −Sextette (with Sembrich, Severina, Scotti, Journet, Daddi)	193	2/08	V 12 96200	10001
†116. −Sextette (with Tetrazzini, Amato, Journet, Jacoby, Bada)	141	1/12	V 12 96201	16-5000
†117. −Sextette (with Galli-Curci, Egener, DeLuca, Journet, Bada)	195	1/17	V 12 95212	10000
118. Luna d'Estate, *Tosti*	155	2/16	V 10 87242	519
119. Luna fedel (piano), *Denza*		1902	ZON 10 1551	
120. Luna fedel (piano), *Denza*		11/02	G&T 10 52442	
MACBETH, *Verdi:*				
121. −Ah, la paterna mano	55	2/16	V 12 88558	6014
MADAMA BUTTERFLY, *Puccini:*				
122. −O quant' occhi fisi (with Farrar)	130	3/08	V 12 89017	8011
123. −Amore o grillo (with Scotti)	124	3/10	V 12 89043	8014
124. −Ve lo dissi? (with Scotti)	123	3/10	V 12 89047	8014
125. Mamma mia che vo sape, *Nutile*	105	11/09	V 12 88206	6009
126. Manella mia, *Valente*	173	1/14	V 12 88465	6025

TITLE AND COMPOSER †INDICATES RECORDS STILL IN PRINT	DOU-BLED WITH	DATE RE-CORDED	MAKE, SIZE AND 1ST NO.	LATER NOS.
MANON, *Massenet:*				
127. –Ah fuyez (French)	95	12/11	V 12 88348	6020
128. –Il sogno (piano)		3/02	G&T 10 52345	
129. –Il sogno (piano)	215	2/04	V 10 81031	523
130. –On l'appelle Manon (French; with Farrar)	122	12/12	V 12 89059	8011
MANON LESCAUT, *Puccini:*				
131. –Donna non vidi mai (harp –Regis-Rossini)	159	2/13	V 10 87135	505
MARTHA, *Flotow:*				
132. –M'appari		2/06	V 12 88001	
†133. –M'appari	221 165	4/17	V 12 88001	6002 7720
134. –Solo profugo (with Journet)	77	1/10	V 12 89036	8016
135. –Che vuol dir ciò? (with Alda, Jacoby, Journet)	138	1/12	V 12 95208	10002
136. –Presto presto (with Alda, Jacoby, Journet)	137	1/12	V 12 95209	10003
†137. –Quartetto notturno (with Alda, Jacoby, Journet)	136 111	1/12	V 12 95210	10003 16-5002
138. –Siam giunti (with Alda, Jacoby, Journet)	135	1/12	V 12 95207	10002
MASKED BALL, *Verdi:*				
139. –Di' tu se fedele	222	11/11	V 10 87091	512
140. –Ma se m'è forza	201	12/11	V 12 88346	6027
†141. –E scherzo (with Hempel, Duchene, Rothier, DeSegurola)	142 116	4/14	V 12 89076	10005 16-500c
142. –La rivedrà (with Hempel, Rothier, DeSegurola)	141	4/14	V 12 89077	10005
143. Mattinata (piano–Leoncavallo), *Leoncavallo*		1902	G&T 10 52034	
MEFISTOFELE, *Boïto:*				
144. –Giunto sul passo (piano)		3/02	G&T 10 52347	
145. –Dai campi (piano)		3/02	G&T 10 52348	matrix no.1789
146. –Dai campi (piano)		1903	G&T 10 52348	matrix no.2871
MESSE SOLONNELLE, *Rossini:*				
147. –Crucifixus (Latin)		9/20	V 10 87335	
148. –Domine Deus (Latin)	6	9/20	V 12 88629	6010
149. Mia canzone (piano), *Tosti* [also issued in United States, 5011, 91010]		11/02	G&T 10 52443	
†150. Mia canzone, *Tosti*	18 25	1/15	V 10 87213	503 1688

TITLE AND COMPOSER †INDICATES RECORDS STILL IN PRINT	DOU-BLED WITH	DATE RE-CORDED	MAKE, SIZE AND 1ST NO.	LATER NOS.
151. Mia sposa sarà la mia bandiera, Rotoli	183	2/16	V 12 88555	6018
152. Milagro de la Virgen (Spanish; piano—Scagnamiglio), Chapi	168	4/14	V 12 6458	
†153. Musica proibita, Gastaldon [also issued on 10-inch later— 2212]	96 1	4/17	V 12 88586	6021
NERON, Rubinstein:				
154. —Ah mon sort (French; harp and orchestra; harp—Lapitino)	67	4/17	V 12 88589	6017
155. Nina, Pergolesi	118	9/19	V 10 87358	519
156. Noche Feliz (Spanish), Posadas	228 7 7	9/20	V 10 958	26571 17-5001
157. Non t'amo più (piano), Denza [also issued in United States, 5014, 91013]		11/02	G&T 10 52441	
†158. O sole mio, Di Capua	233 187	2/16	V 10 87243	501 1616
OTELLO, Verdi:				
159. —Ora e per sempre addio	131	12/10	V 10 87071	505
†160. —Sì, pel ciel (with Ruffo)	*	1/14	V 12 89075	8045
161. Over there (first verse English; second verse French), Cohan	87	7/18	V 10 87294	515
PAGLIACCI, Leoncavallo:				
†162. —No! Pagliaccio non son	165	12/10	V 12 88279	6001
163. —Vesti la giubba (piano— Leoncavallo) [also issued in United States, 5016, 91014]		11/02	G&T 10 52440	
164. —Vesti la giubba (piano)	62	2/04	V 10 81032	930
†165. —Vesti la giubba	162 133	3/07	V 12 88061	6001 7720
166. Parted (English), Tosti	113	3/14	V 10 87186	510
167. Partida (Spanish; piano), Alvarez		4/14	12 2-062003	HMV-DB639
168. Partida (Spanish), Alvarez	152	7/18	V 12 6458	
PEARL FISHERS, Bizet:				
169. —De mon amie (French)	204	12/16	V 10 87269	513
170. —Mi par d'udir (piano— Cottone)	29	1903	G&T 12 052066 IRCC 12 61	
†171. —Je crois (French)	197 12	12/16	V 12 88580	6026 7770
172. —Del tempio al limitar (with Ancona)	53	3/07	V 12 89007	8036
173. Pe'che?, Pennino	126	1/15	V 12 88517	6025

*With Victor 8045: Ruffo—Otello—Credo.

TITLE AND COMPOSER †INDICATES RECORDS STILL IN PRINT	DOU-BLED WITH	DATE RE-CORDED	MAKE, SIZE AND 1ST NO.	LATER NOS.
174. Pietà, Signore, *Attributed to* Stradella	34	9/18	V 12 88599	6024
175. Pimpinella (piano—Scogna-miglio), *Tschaikowsky*	232	1/13	V 10 87128	518
176. Pourquoi? (French), *Tschaikowsky*	177	11/16	V 10 87271	517
177. Pour un baiser (French), *Tosti*	176	11/09	V 10 87042	517
178. Première caresse (French), *Crescenzo*	19	9/19	V 10 1437	
†179. Procession (French), *Franck*	181 182	2/16	V 12 88556	6035 14744
QUEEN OF SHEBA, *Goldmark:*				
180. –Magiche note	205	3/08	V 10 87041	520
QUEEN OF SHEBA, *Gounod:*				
†181. –Prête-moi ton aide (French)	179 40	2/16	V 12 88552	6035 15732
†182. Rameaux (French), *J. Faure*	100 179	3/14	V 12 88459	6022 14744
183. Régiment de Sambre et Meuse (French), *Planquette*	151	1/19	V 12 88600	6018
REQUIEM MASS, *Verdi:*				
184. –Ingemisco (Latin)	208	1/15	V 12 88514	6028
RIGOLETTO, *Verdi:*				
185. –La donna è mobile (piano)		1902	ZON 10 1555	
186. –La donna è mobile (piano)	190	2/04	V 10 81026	522
†187. –La donna è mobile	191 158	3/08	V 10 87017	500 1616
†188. –Parmi veder le lagrime	64 64	2/13	V 12 88429	6016 11-8112
189. –Questa o quella (piano)		3/02	G&T 10 52344	
190. –Questa o quella (piano)	186	2/04	V 10 81025	522
191. –Questa o quella	187	3/08	V 10 87018	500
192. –Quartet (with Abbott, Homer, Scotti)	74	2/07	V 12 96000	10011
†193. –Quartet (with Sembrich, Severina, Scotti)	115 32	2/08	V 12 96001	10001 16-5001
194. –Quartet (with Tetrazzini, Jacoby, Amato) [not on regular Victor release]	*	2/12	IRCC 12 36	
†195. –Quartet (with Galli-Curci, Perini, DeLuca)	117	1/17	V 12 95100	10000
SALVATOR ROSA, *Gomez:*				
196. –Mia piccirella	66	9/19	V 12 88638	6034
SAMSON AND DELILAH, *Saint-Saëns:*				
197. –Vois ma misère (French)	171	12/16	V 12 88581	6026

*With IRCC 36: *Destinn and Kirkby-Lunn—Aïda.*

TITLE AND COMPOSER †INDICATES RECORDS STILL IN PRINT	DOU-BLED WITH	DATE RE-CORDED	MAKE, SIZE AND 1ST NO.	LATER NOS.
†198. –Je viens célébrer (French; with Homer and Journet)	111 73	2/19	V 12 89088	10010 16-5003
199. Sancta Maria (French), J. Faure	36	3/16	V 12 88559	6029
200. Santa Lucia, Folksong	49	3/16	V 12 88560	6032
SCHIAVO, Gomez:				
201. –Quando nascesti tu	140	11/11	V 12 88345	6027
202. Scordame, Fucito	203	9/19	V 10 1007	
203. Senza nisciuno, De Curtis	202	9/19	V 10 1007	
204. Sérénade de Don Juan (French), Tschaikowsky	169	1/14	V 10 87175	513
205. Sérénade Espagnole (French), Ronald	180	3/14	V 10 87169	520
206. Seranata, Bracco	211	9/19	V 12 88628	6033
207. Si vous l'aviez compris (French; piano–Scognamiglio; violin–Elman), Denza	52	2/15	V 12 89084	8008
STABAT MATER, Rossini:				
208. –Cujus animam (Latin)	184	12/13	V 12 88460	6028
209. Sultanto a te, Fucito	231	2/19	V 10 1117	
210. Tarantella Sincera, Crescenzo	51	12/11	V 12 88347	6031
211. Tiempo antico, Caruso	206	3/16	V 12 88472	6033
TOSCA, Puccini:				
212. –E lucevan le stelle (piano) Also on Pathé cylinder Also issued on Emerson cut		1898-99 ca.1918	P 14 84004 E 6 301	
213. –E lucevan le stelle (piano)		1902	ZON 10 1553	
214. –E lucevan le stelle (piano) [also issued in United States, 5010, 91009]		3/02	G&T 10 52349	
215. –E lucevan le stelle (piano)	129	2/04	V 10 81028	523
216. –E lucevan le stelle	218	11/09	V 10 87044	511
217. –Recondita armonia (piano)		2/04	V 10 81029	
†218. –Recondita armonia [also issued on 12-inch–11-8569]	216*	11/09	V 10 87043	511
TRAVIATA, Verdi:				
219. –Brindisi (with Gluck)	222	4/14	V 10 87511	3031
220. Triste ritorno, Barthelemy	230	12/06	V 12 88048	6030
TROVATORE, Verdi:				
221. –Ah sì, ben mio	133	3/08	V 12 88121	6002
222. –Di quella pira	139 219	2/06	V 10 87001	512 3031
†223. –Miserere (with Alda)	225	12/09	V 12 89030	8042
224. –Ai nostri monti (with Homer)	226	3/08	V 12 89018	8013
†225. –Ai nostri monti (with Schumann-Heink)	223	1/13	V 12 89060	8042
226. –Mal reggendo (with Homer)	224	12/10	V 12 89049	8013

*Also with Victor 11-8569: Bori–Traviata–Sempre libera.

TITLE AND COMPOSER †INDICATES RECORDS STILL IN PRINT	DOU-BLED WITH	DATE RE-CORDED	MAKE, SIZE AND 1ST NO.	LATER NOS.
227. Trusting eyes (English), *Gartner*	234	3/14	V 10 87187	514
228. Tu ca nun chiagne, *De Curtis*	156	9/19	V 10 958	
†229. Tu non mi vuoi più bene (piano), *Composer unknown*		1898-99	P 14 84003	
Also on Pathé cylinder				
Also on regular cut C.R.S.	103 C.R.S.		C.R.S. 10 6	
230. Uocchio celeste, *Crescenzo*	220	4/17	V 12 88587	6030
231. Vaghissima sembianza, *Donaudy*	209	9/20	V 10 1117	
232. Vieni sul mar, *Composer unknown*	175	9/19	V 10 87305	518
233. A vucchella, *Tosti*	158	9/19	V 10 87304	501
234. Your eyes have told me (English), *O'Hara*	227	7/13	V 10 87159	514

ABOUT THE AUTHOR

DOROTHY PARK BENJAMIN CARUSO, *born of generations of New York-*
ers, has spent most of her life in France and Italy. During the first
years of the war she remained in France to help clothe and feed hun-
dreds of destitute families in the Alpes Maritimes. She returned to
New York in 1942.

Her grandfather, Park Benjamin, was a newspaper publisher, lec-
turer, associate editor with Horace Greeley of The New Yorker and
friend of Poe, Longfellow, and Oliver Wendell Holmes. Her father,
also Park Benjamin, in addition to being a writer on scientific sub-
jects and editor of The Scientific American, was well known as a
patent lawyer.

Dorothy Caruso's early years were spent in private schools in New
York City. At thirteen she was sent to a convent of the Sacred Heart.
In 1917 she met Enrico Caruso and knew at once, as he did, that they
would marry. Within a few months they eloped. Two years later their
daughter, Gloria, was born. Their life together was fabulously happy
until Caruso was stricken with an illness which ended fatally in
Naples in 1921.

"In writing this book," says Dorothy Caruso, "I have faithfully re-
corded every word and action of Enrico which might interpret him
to the public—not only to those who were privileged to hear him sing
but also to those who were not yet born when he died.

"When I returned to this country I found that Enrico was not for-
gotten but living as if he had never died. Twenty-five years is a long

302

time but my memory of him is as clear as if he had left me an hour ago. With every word I wrote he walked into the room. The more I wrote, the more clear those years became.

"I never reread his letters after his death. I never looked at them until I began the book and realized that they were the best illustration of his thought. Because he was such a silent man and thought before he spoke, I think I have remembered everything he said.

"I suppose this book has been composing itself in me for years. It has given me an opportunity not only to correct false legends which have distressed me, but also to affirm Enrico's dimensions as a human being."